BLUE ROOTS

BLUE ROOTS

AFRICAN-AMERICAN FOLK MAGIC
OF THE GULLAH PEOPLE

SECOND EDITION

~

ROGER PINCKNEY

SANDLAPPER PUBLISHING CO., INC.
ORANGEBURG, SOUTH CAROLINA 29115

SECOND EDITION
ISBN 978-0-87844-168-6
Second Printing, 2007

Previous edition (ISBN 1-56718-524-X) published by
     Llewellyn Publications, © 1998 Roger Pinckney

This edition published by Sandlapper Publishing Co., Inc.
     Orangeburg, South Carolina 29115

Photographs on pages 2, 6, 13, 37, 38, 65, 104, and 106 used by permission. All other photographs by the author.

Manufactured in the United States of America

Library of Congress Cataloging-in-Publication Data

Pinckney, Roger, 1946–
   Blue roots : African-American folk magic of the Gullah people / Roger
Pinckney.— 2nd ed.
       p. cm.
   Includes bibliographical references and index.
   ISBN 0-87844-168-9 (pbk. : alk. paper)
   1. Gullahs—Folklore. 2. African American magic—South
Carolina—Saint Helena Island. 3. Voodooism—South Carolina—Saint
Helena Island. 4. Folklore—South Carolina—Saint Helena Island.   I.
Title.
GR111.A47P56 2003
398'.09757'59—dc22

                                                           2003016291

Discover the Power
of "The Root"

One August we entered a sweltering shanty on Coosaw Island. Inside, the family huddled around a battered pine table, staring silently at the light of a single, flickering kerosene lamp. From the back room came a groan, then a regular *thump, thump, thump* in steady cadence. My grandmother strode across the kitchen floor and threw open the bedroom door.

A man lay on a filthy, unmade cot, glistening with deathsweat—his eyes rolled back in his head—moaning, bucking, writhing. There was an explosion of explanation from the women. "The hags gottem, Miz Martin," one of the younger ones blurted, "an' we ain't know what to do!"

The old matriarch related the circumstances of her man's expected demise. There had been a long-standing feud with one of their island neighbors, exacerbated by unclear property lines and wandering and garden-trampling livestock. The woman expected the neighbors had "rooted" her husband when a series of unexplained minor misfortunes beset them. But the man paid no attention until the hags set to riding him one night. "We saw off de bedposts, so they can't roost, but it ain' done no good," the woman said, throwing up her hands in resignation. "Jesus have 'em by an' by."

Dedication

For all those people, black and white,
that it took to raise me.

Contents

BLUE ROOTS

An Introduction

It has been often said that those hapless occupants of seventeenth- and eighteenth-century slave ships carried nothing with them on their involuntary journeys from their native West Africa to the New World.

This is not true. Though they were stripped of everything but their names, Africans newly impressed into slavery carried fragmented memories of their culture—music, folklore, social structure, and religion—to the mines and plantations of the Americas. Disease and cruel overwork condemned many to their deaths in Central and South America. But on the plantations of the American South, the slaves multiplied and passed their African roots to their descendants in a rich and lasting oral tradition, a tradition that survives to this day.

Though few accurate records were kept of the numbers prior to 1806—when legal slave importation was prohibited by Federal law—some modern historians estimate that no more than 250,000 slaves were imported, mostly through Charleston, Savannah, New Orleans, and Annapolis. It is one of history's more curious facts that some 30,000,000 living African-Americans trace their ancestry to those relatively few original slaves.

Bay Street, looking east. Beaufort, South Carolina.
Courtesy of South Caroliniana Library, University of South Carolina, Columbia.

The sea islands of the South Carolina and Georgia coast provided a fertile environment for the survival of West African culture. Overseen by a small number of whites, the slaves worked on vast island plantations isolated from the mainland, on moist and verdant ground, not entirely unlike the lands from which they had been taken.

African medicine men, erroneously called "witch doctors" by the whites, whose prophesies or remedies failed to impress local chieftains were also sold into slavery and added to this potent mix. Though their efforts were sometimes repressed by worried slaveowners, the rhythm of African drums often echoed through the Carolina and Geor-

gia night.

As part of an English royal colony, Beaufort's St. Helena's Parish—the focus of *Blue Roots*—was supplied Episcopal ministers at government expense. Early Methodists and Baptists, known in those days as "dissenters," faulted Episcopal ministers and large plantations owners for not suppressing native African beliefs. Baptists set aside one Sunday each month for a special Negro church service, and the Methodists sent out missionaries who urged planters to allow them to hold at least one service per month on each plantation.

Typical of early missionaries was Methodist reverend Thomas E. Ledbetter. Ledbetter traveled throughout the coastal Lowcountry, where he tried to purge the plantation slave subculture of its African heritage, believing it incompatible with Christian beliefs.

Most slaves thought otherwise. Though they enthusiastically accepted baptism, they were quite unwilling to completely forego their native beliefs and continued to consult traditional practitioners whenever they deemed it appropriate for both emotional and physical health, as well as for less benign reasons: success or revenge.

By 1836, Ledbetter was about to give up, declaring, ". . . we combat a great many false notions, fatal doctrines . . . through ignorant and superstitious teachers. And nothing is more difficult to overcome than a strongly prejudiced understanding. . . ."

Baptism on Daufuskie Island, South Carolina. Locals baptize on the falling tide, so the river will carry sin out to sea.

Shortly after the first shots of the Civil War, the coasts of South Carolina and Georgia fell to the U.S. Navy. Slaveowners fled the area, and tens of thousands of newly freed slaves flocked to the Federal authorities for protection and sustenance. Burdened by the care of so many, the government established numerous freedmen on land confiscated from their former masters. The promise of "forty acres and a mule" turned out to be considerably less—from ten to twenty-five acres and no mules.

But hundreds of families received deeds in the only egalitarian land redistribution scheme in U.S. history. The

government briefly employed Northerners to teach agriculture, citizenship, and literacy. But once the shooting stopped, many teachers went back north and the freedmen resumed lives close to the soil, as isolated as ever.

These African-American communities survived intact and unmolested well into the twentieth century, retaining much of the language and many of the beliefs of the slave

African-American traditions survived intact well into the twentieth century, and beyond.

Lady's Island cabin.
Courtesy of South Caroliniana Library, University of South Carolina,
Columbia.

days. Folklorists and linguists identified them as Gullah, a term that may have been derived from Angola, on the southwest coast of Africa. Prominent among Gullah culture was the belief in herbalism, spiritualism, and black magic. While in other places this belief was called "ubia," "voodoo," or "santeria," the Gullah called it "the root."

The "root" was a charm, a "mojo" or "gris-gris" as it was known in New Orleans. Most roots were cloth sacks the size of a pecan. Others were liquids contained in small vi-

als. Roots were administered or removed by a root doctor, a practitioner, who in later years wore blue sunglasses and generally took the name of an animal. There was Dr. Bug, Dr. Fly, Dr. Crow, Dr. Snake, Dr. Turtle, and the infamous Dr. Buzzard.

Dr. Buzzard's real name was Stephaney Robinson. He held sway for nearly forty years, beginning in the early 1900s in the Gullah community on St. Helena Island, South Carolina, around the isolated hamlet of Frogmore. Dr. Buzzard not only sold roots to a nationwide clientele that numbered in the thousands and predicted winning numbers in clandestine lotteries, he was reputed to have spirits at his command—various haunts and hags that flitted around the edges of island reality. If Dr. Buzzard put an evil root on a man, locals said, that man was as good as dead.

I was born in 1946 on Port Royal Island, in the town of Beaufort, South Carolina, and came of age in the '50s and '60s, just in time to see the old ways pass.

There are some thirteen inhabited islands among the nearly 400 that lie like emeralds in the frothy and passionate blue of the Atlantic edge. Those islands had been thoroughly discovered—first by the Spanish in 1521, then in succession by the French, English, Scots, Confederates, Yankees, and lastly by hordes of northern urbanites who were fleeing the pollution and random mayhem of their native streets.

The northerners came in droves. Sea Pines Plantation

on nearby Hilton Head was the first incursion. Thousands of acres of maritime forest were bulldozed into golf courses, tennis courts, and quarter-million-dollar lots. The original development at Sea Pines was fairly well planned and centered around several thousand acres of timberland. Its resounding financial success brought a dozen immediate competitors—as well as haphazard development, environmental degradation, and the eventual uprooting of much of Beaufort County's long time population, Gullah and whites alike. In 20 years Beaufort County's population doubled. It had taken 250 years to double the last time.

Skyrocketing land values caused a proportionate rise in property taxes, while most jobs at the new resorts paid only minimum wage. Hundreds sold land they could no longer afford to own—some, land that had been in the family for a century. A case in point: A local well driller was called to a remote island location where an aged Gullah man, living alone, nearly blind, was out of water. The man offered to trade "de crick acres" for a new well, pump, and a single cold water faucet in his pitiful kitchen. The well driller did the work as directed, had his lawyer prepare a quitclaim deed upon which the old man scrawled his name.

But then the trouble began. There was $500 in tax arrearages, ten times that amount for a surveyor. Since land in the Gullah community had been passed from parents to children without benefit of wills, there was an astounding $7,000 legal bill for clear title. When the county assessor

got wind of the proceedings, he tripled the property tax. Two years later, the driller was eager to sell. He found a man from New Jersey who was willing to pay $80,000 for the eight "crick acres." The driller gloated for a single week, until the New Jersey speculator resold it for $180,000.

Meanwhile, the tax bill on the old man's remaining acres drove him from the land. He spent his last years in a "coloreds only" nursing home fifty miles away, which, after the man's lingering death, filed a lien against the property to settle the substantial bill for the man's care. They subsequently executed judgement, greased the wheels of justice to clear the title, then midway through the proceedings, sold their interest to a Massachusetts investor's group. A local wag proclaimed, "The first Yankee invasion stole the white man's land; the second stole the Gullah's."

To be sure, much was gained. The schools were desegregated, county health officials finally contained rampant hookworm, syphilis, and tuberculosis, as well as occasional outbreaks of scurvy, beri-beri, and obscure African diseases that had no English names. Most islands got bridges, all got electricity. People went to work and bought washing machines, refrigerators, televisions.

But much was lost. Well-meaning teachers told students their Gullah heritage was an impediment to success in white society. Gullah children, in their efforts to please, tried to talk like the man on the six o'clock news. Most professed ignorance of the old ways—especially the ways of the root

and the root doctor. Unbelievers were afraid whites would remember their grandparents were held under the sway of island voodoo. Believers were simply afraid talk would conjure up unwanted spiritual visitations. It would be nearly thirty years before a local Gullah festival attempted to salvage what few memories were left.

My paternal grandmother was orphaned at an early age and perhaps bore childhood scars into an adulthood of nervous compulsion. Weak in both flesh and spirit, she suffered an emotional and physical collapse after the birth of each child. During these self-imposed periods of stasis, she employed Elvira Mike, a Gullah woman who helped raise my father, his five brothers and sisters, my two older cousins, and, finally, me. I thought her old enough to have wed Methuselah. And when I learned that as a child she had seen the battleship *Maine* take on coal at the Port Royal Naval Station on its way to destiny in Havana, I was sure of it.

Family legends say this: Elvira completed the third grade before reporting to work in "de patch," one of the many local truck farms that grew cucumbers, melons, and tomatoes for the New York market. Her scant literacy allowed her to decipher a census taker's report that pronounced her illegitimate. When she asked her mother the meaning of the word, her mother coyly replied, "It's when she chile ain't have she father name." Elvira remembered

the deficiency and, upon reaching her maturity, successfully petitioned District Court to have her last name changed to Mike, the name she remembered her mother calling her father.

At an early age, Elvira took me upon her knee, told me stories, sang spirituals sprung with the syncopated rhythm of the African village. Sometimes, when the spirit moved her, she would ease me onto the floor, leap to her feet, and dance "shouts"—the old dances of praise to a God who was as fully black as he was white. I followed her, jigging, stamping, clapping, shouting as best I could. She lived well into her nineties, old enough to have my own children also crawl upon her lap. Though by then she was far too old to dance, my children heard the stories and the songs.

My maternal grandmother was Chlotilde Rowell, who in 1919, as a recent college graduate, accepted a job with *The State* newspaper in the capital city of Columbia, becoming the first female reporter in South Carolina history allowed to write beyond the society page. Though her presence in the office severely annoyed rough talking, tobacco chewing male journalists, my grandmother soon proved her mettle when she was the only reporter volunteering to fly with Eddie Rickenbacker, the World War I ace who was making a triumphal nationwide victory tour in his biplane. Her stint aloft impressed the man who was to become my grandfather. No-longer-skeptical office mate Thomas S. Martin began passing love notes beneath the partition that sepa-

rated their desks.

That correspondence was successful and the newlywed Martins worked first at *The Beaufort Gazette*, then moved up-state to run *The Greenwood Index-Journal*. After the untimely death of my grandfather from lymphatic cancer, Chlotilde Rowell Martin brought her two young children—my mother and my uncle—to Beaufort where she served as a long-time correspondent for the Charleston *News and Courier*.

A freelance writer's life is always hard. Being a female freelancer during the Depression with two small children to raise was even harder. My grandmother took a part-time job with the South Carolina Department of Welfare and was as-signed to travel the remote islands to interview potential benefit recipients. I tagged along at an early age, serving as her "navigator," as she called me, poring over maps, deci-phering scribbled directions, staring out the windows of her 1956 Chevrolet in big-eyed wonder as Gullah ferrymen barged us across dark singing waters, as we passed ox and pony carts on the rutted sandy tracks of island roads.

It was on one of these excursions I first encountered the power of the root. One August we entered a sweltering shanty on Coosaw Island, a shanty that had window frames and door posts painted blue to keep spirits at bay, a shanty with windows tightly closed as if to keep something out—or something in. The family—an aged matriarchal crone, fully grown daughters, a half dozen grandchildren, and a scatter-ing of great-grandchildren—huddled around a battered pine

table staring silently at the light of a single, flickering kero-sene lamp. From the back room came a groan, then a regu-lar *thump, thump, thump* in steady cadence. My grandmother, still possessing the spirit that sent her aloft with Eddie Rickenbacker, strode across the kitchen floor and threw open the bedroom door.

A man lay on a filthy unmade cot, glistening with deathsweat—eyes rolled back in his head—moaning, bucking, writhing. There was an explosion of explanation from the women. "The hags gottem, Miz Martin," one of the younger

Ox cart on St. Helena Island road.
Courtesy of South Caroliniana Library, University of South Carolina, Columbia.

ones blurted, "an' we ain't know what to do!" The old matriarch related the circumstances of her man's expected demise. There had been a long-standing feud with one of their
island neighbors, exacerbated by unclear property lines and
wandering and garden-trampling livestock. The woman expected the neighbors had "rooted" her husband when a series of inexplicable minor misfortunes beset them. But the
man paid no attention until the hags set to riding him one
night. "We saw off de bedposts, so they can't roost, but it
ain' done no good," the woman said, throwing up her
hands in resignation. "Jesus have 'em by an' by."

Though I am unable to remember the outcome of that
particular hex, I have no doubt the old woman's prediction
was entirely correct.

There was my father, Roger Pinckney, the tenth in a
long line of first sons to bear that name. Roger X wore two
hats. He was "Capum Roger," a marine contractor who—
with a crew of Gullah laborers—built docks, bridges, and
seawalls. He also served as coroner of Beaufort County for
thirty-six years. Sprinkled in with the grisly parade of auto
wrecks, drownings, murders, and suicides, came occasional
and inexplicable deaths from root and hex.

Being coroner required a certain hardening of sensibili-
ties and the passing years calloused those few he retained
until, as one of his workmen succinctly told me, "Yo pappy
can set plate on dead man's face an' eat he supper."

But he remembered all he saw and as I grew older, he

often related the more outrageous episodes, tales that haunt me still, as they must have haunted him.

And there was J. E. McTeer, High Sheriff of the Lowcountry, close friend of my father who, for some reason, took a special interest in me as a boy. In 1926, at the tender age of twenty-two, McTeer had been sworn in to fill the vacancy left by the death of his father. His friends called him Ed. Somewhat-skeptical local politicians dubbed him "the boy sheriff." But the Gullah community, distinguishing him from a number of lesser deputies, called him "the High Sheriff."

The High Sheriff had experience with the supernatural dating from his boyhood. There was an old Gullah woman living on his father's farm and young Ed McTeer had teased her incessantly about needing a husband. The woman retaliated by threatening to return and "hant" the young man after her death. Several months after the old woman's funeral, young Ed was passing the cemetery on his pony at dusk and, remembering the threat, closed his eyes so if any spirit arose from the grave, he would not see it. The pony, however, kept his open and apparently saw something. It spooked, bucked, and sent the young man sprawling over the fresh mound of graveyard dirt. Ed's mother remarked that he outran the pony, arriving home well before the lathered and shaking animal.

Once he became sheriff, young Ed encountered the work of local root doctors, who often crossed the shadowy

line between legal and illegal activities in efforts on their clients' behalf. To counter these activities, Ed decided to begin a serious study of rootwork, reading everything he could find on African history and tribal traditions.

But the High Sheriff's experience was far from academic. After learning the basics, he began to spread the word that he was a practitioner himself. That assertion first bore fruit in an instance described by Arthur Paul, the father of my neighbor and fishing buddy, who was a good friend and fishing buddy of the High Sheriff.

According to Paul, he and Ed McTeer were returning from a fishing venture on one of the local estuaries. There came a garbled call on the radio, and the High Sheriff asked his friend's permission to divert from their intended direction to attend to "a little business."

"We drove up into the yard of one of those island beer joints," Paul told me. "Ed got out and went inside." But no sooner than the High Sheriff had cleared the threshold, the lights went out and gunfire broke loose. Arthur Paul recalled seeing the flashes in the darkened windows and holding his head in his hands. "He's dead!" he cried to himself. "Ed's dead!"

But a minute later, the lights went back on and Ed McTeer emerged, hauling the suspect by the scruff of the neck. A subsequent tally showed the suspect's gun had been emptied and the High Sheriff claimed his weapon had never left its holster.

Word of that incident spread like wildfire across swamp, island, and field, with the supposition that black magic had made the High Sheriff bulletproof. It was a misconception that was to serve him well. His adversaries were terrified of his powers. On another occasion, after he was shot at while arresting a burglary suspect, he refused to let the prosecutor add attempted murder to the long list of charges pending against the suspect. When asked for an explanation, the High Sheriff's considerable vanity slipped into overdrive, "There was no murder attempted, since he had no chance of hitting me. I'd stand the length of this courtroom and let a Gullah shoot at me all day!"

Ed McTeer lived, appropriately, on an island plantation bearing the name of Coffin Point. There were a couple of coveys of half-tame bobwhite quail darting around the outbuildings that served to educate chosen local boys in the finer points of shotgunnery—missing, mostly. As a teenager, those quail tried both my eye and my patience. I don't remember downing very many of them, but I do remember the after-hunt sessions in the High Sheriff's library, where I sat among African masks and totems, sipping Dixie Colas and soaking up his endless repertory of tales.

These, then, are stories of haunts, hags, the dreaded spirit called the *plateye*, root doctors, spells, and hexes, as they were told by people who loved me . . . and what I have learned since.

Out of Africa

Though the sins of the white race are innumerable, the invention of slavery is not among them. Slavery existed in Africa long before the first white incursions into what Europeans called, in their typical *hubris*, "the dark continent." The great sin of the white race was, and is, its ability, through mechanization, economic and political power, to do evil on so vast a scale. Murder became genocide, war became annihilation, hunting became extinction, humankind's inevitable impact on its surroundings became global environmental degradation. And tribal and individual holding of slaves became an institution, an international trade, a pervasive social institution. So great was its impact, historians estimate that by 1850, fully one-third of the world's people of African descent were living outside Africa.

The first Africans imported into what was to become the United States occurred in 1612 at Jamestown, Virginia, with the arrival of a Dutch ship with "twenty neegars," according to a colonial journal. A century later, Charles Town (Charleston), Colony of Carolina, had become the center of the North American slave trade. Still, numbers were small, ranging from 24 in 1706 to 604 in 1724.

Most of these first slaves were "Guinea Negroes," ethnic Wolofs and Mendes from northwest Africa, who were utilized for household work. Because they worked in close proximity to their masters (and often mistresses) they were quickly assimilated into the majority culture. But that was about to change.

Since the colonies, especially the Carolinas and Georgia, depended on English-manufactured goods, a medium of exchange had to be developed to raise the cash needed for economic survival. The northern colonies had abundant water power, which would eventually be used in industrial applications, but the South had to rely on the exportation of raw products. Forest products, called "marine stores" from their importance in shipbuilding, were the major exports from Georgia and the Carolinas. Sturdy oak for ship's planking, tall pines for masts, turpentine and pitch for caulking made England an international maritime power. But once the great forests were cleared and land freed up for cultivation, a number of agricultural crops surpassed logging. Among them were tobacco, indigo, rice, and cotton.

Tobacco was first brought back to England by Sir Walter Raleigh in the late sixteenth century. Smoked in long clay pipes, its use soon became widespread throughout Europe. Indigo was processed into a rich blue dye and used to color cloth turned out by English mills and exported worldwide. But tobacco was cultivated in small plots, primarily in the Virginia midlands. Though its harvest was labor intensive, it was profitable without slave labor. Colonial indigo planters enjoyed a monopoly under English law, an advantage that was lost with independence in 1776. The price subsequently collapsed and planters turned to other crops, primarily rice and cotton.

Rice seed had been brought to South Carolina from the African island of Madagascar prior to the Revolution. Large cypress swamps and extensive freshwater marshes just inland from the coastal tidal zone were ideal for its cultivation, but preparation of the land and cultivation of the crop made a large labor force mandatory. Towering cypress had to be cut, the stumps grubbed out, canals dug, and dikes and flood control structures built. The land was drained and dried for cultivation, planted, then flooded. Just prior to harvest, fields were drained again, then the rice cut, bunched, and bundled by hand. Rice was threshed and milled first by hand, later by horse and hand-powered machinery, bagged, then barged downstream to Charleston and Savannah where it was loaded onto sailing ships and transported worldwide.

Growing cotton, likewise, required a massive infusion of labor. Cotton was planted, cultivated, and picked by hand. It was also hard on the land. After only three or four years of continuous cropping, yields were noticeably reduced. This meant new land had to be constantly cleared or the old land refurnished with nutrients through the spreading of animal or crop wastes—or in some cases, with heavy river mud. Even after the invention of Whitney's mechanical cotton gin in the early 1800s, the long-fibered "sea island cotton" cultivated along the coast was processed by hand. The delicate fibers broke and knotted in the gins or became so hot from the working of the machine it yellowed and was discounted at market.

By the mid-1700s, many of South Carolina and Georgia's whites had come to think of themselves as members of an aristocracy. The first settlers had come from plantation families in the British West Indies. Subsequent arrivals were the second and third sons of English gentry, prohibited by law from inheriting their fathers' estates, who chose emigration to America as the lesser of three bad options, the other two being the priesthood and the army. They looked aghast at shovel, hoe, and adze. They would sweat enthusiastically in love and sport, but arduous physical labor was far below their station in life. Resident Indians made poor slaves and had already been decimated by contact with white diseases. There were a few indentured servants—poor Englishmen who had bound themselves to a

master for seven years in exchange for ocean passage. But these were mostly tradesmen—cobblers, carpenters, blacksmiths—far too valuable for field work. And so the job fell, by default, to those who had no choice in the matter: African slaves. White planters rationalized their dependence on slave labor in other ways as well. Africans had nothing in their native land and would benefit from association with whites. Some might learn to read, most would be Christianized. Half a lifetime in slavery would be a small price to pay for Eternal Salvation. Besides, there were more realistic considerations. Africans were used to the tropics and thought to be immune to malaria and yellow fever, two mosquito-borne diseases that had laid low many colonial whites.

This is how it worked. Ships laden with raw products—tobacco, indigo, rice, and West Indian sugar—made an ocean crossing to English ports where their cargoes were sold. They were loaded with manufactured goods—muskets, knives, pots and pans, rum, and the inevitable beads, trinkets, and baubles. Then they sailed for Africa where the goods were traded for human cargoes—called "black ivory" from the extreme profitability of the trade.

Since slavery—the ownership of Africans by other Africans—was long established in Africa, the first slaves taken to America were from a slave caste, slaves who were the sons and daughters, even the grandsons and granddaughters, of slaves. But that supply was quickly exhausted and coastal tribes were supplied guns and rum and encouraged to make

war on their neighbors in the interior. The captives from those wars became slaves of the victors and, ultimately, slaves of Englishmen and Americans. Statistics from colonial treasury reports trace that mayhem's march into the interior. Prior to the 1730s, most slaves imported into the Carolinas were coastal Africans, primarily the aforementioned Wolofs and Mendes. From 1735 to 1740, sixty percent originated from Angola and Central Africa, mostly ethnic Bantus.

These later imports taken in inter-tribal wars encouraged by white slavers were, in effect, political prisoners from a warrior-priest caste. They were steeped in their culture and well educated in their respective tribe's socio-religious traditions, primarily in the *Ifa* beliefs of the dominant Yoruba nation. Though the Yorubas, from present-day Nigeria, had suffered a political collapse under the predations of Arab and European slave traders, their culture remained largely intact. And that culture was to have a profound and lasting impact on African-American belief.

Whites, incidentally, seldom ventured into the interior on these slaving expeditions. Fearing disease and retribution, whites waited at "slave factories," coastal cities, or islands just offshore, in ships bearing such benign names as *Southwind* and *Brotherhood,* while their proxies did their dirty work ashore. Then the ships made their crossing to America to begin the cycle again.

The misery of that crossing is unimaginable. Three to five hundred men and women, chained together, lying in

fear, filth, and darkness as the ship pitched and rolled for three, sometimes four, weeks, taken from the only lives they had ever known, heading for an uncertain future. They had ceased to be people. They had become property. And, as property, they had a monetary value. Slave captains did not want them to die. They were fed minimum rations—mostly vegetable gruel cooked in the ships galley—and, in fair weather, were taken up onto the deck for air and exercise. Still, slavers expected mortality. Ten percent, even twenty percent, of the slaves might perish before the voyage became unprofitable. Efforts were taken to minimize loss. Those who succumbed were unceremoniously thrown overboard to the schools of sharks that always followed slave ships.

Once in America, the slaves were pawed over by anxious buyers, mouthed like horses, auctioned like cattle. A curious belief system sprung up among whites as to the suitability of various ethnic groups for various jobs. Africans from the northwest—Gambians and Senegalese—were thought to be more intelligent because of an old infusion of Arabic blood. These slaves were retained for household duties, taught crafts and trades, or given authority over other slaves. Mandingos were loyal but tended to thievery. Whydahs were cheerful and did not overly resent whipping. Angolans were strong and long-suffering—perfect for field work. But the slaves most prized by coastal planters were the very few from Madagascar, for these Africans knew how to grow rice better than others, including the planters themselves.

African contributions to American culture has been widely overlooked by modern Eurocentric historians. Most Africans, to be sure, owned little in their native land—a few possessions, perhaps a piece of land. But Africans came from essentially oral cultures. If they desired to remember something, they did not—and could not—write it down. Skills, songs, stories, religious beliefs were passed verbally down the generations and committed to memory. Although the slaves may have been stripped of everything but the most essential clothing, they retained their most valuable assets: their memories. And they surely did not suffer collective cultural amnesia the moment they stepped off the boat in Charleston or Savannah.

Senegambian basket weaving serves as an outstanding metaphor for massive cultural retention. Gullah women in the Charleston area weave distinctive baskets of sweetgrass, palmetto, and pine straw and offer them for sale to tourists at dozens of stands strung out along U.S. Highway 17. Though today sold primarily for decorations, these

baskets were once in daily use throughout the Carolina Lowcountry. And they are identical to baskets made and used in Senegal, on Africa's northwest coast. There had been no direct contact between the cultures for over one hundred and fifty years. There are no books on basket weaving on either side of the ocean. If this knowledge, this simple skill, has been simultaneously maintained, passed down innumerable generations, what else has survived?

The answer is obviously a lot—quite a lot.

Women continue to weave sweetgrass baskets in the stylistic tradition of their ancestors.

CHAPTER TWO

God's People in Babylon

In spite of slaveholders' contention that slavery was beneficial because it allowed the Christianization of large numbers of Africans, there was initially little effort to preach the Gospel to slaves. Some household slaves—"servants," as they were euphemistically called—absorbed Christianity from their close contact with devout masters. Others followed their families to the services at Anglican—later Episcopal—churches, as witnessed by names carved in balcony benches and railings in Beaufort's St. Helena's, built in 1724 and used continuously until the Civil War invasion of 1861, when slave owners abandoned the area and the building was converted to a hospital.

Baptists and Methodists were somewhat more evangelical than their more genteel Episcopal neighbors. Men like

Beaufort's William "Good Billy" Fripp brought not only his household slaves but often dozens of field hands to Baptist services. Itinerant ministers, mostly Baptists and Methodists, travelled the plantation country, urging owners to allow them to hold a special service for slaves at least one Sunday each month. They seemed to have made little headway with these requests, as the white population was divided as to whether Africans possessed souls worthy of redemption. Indeed, even the basic humanity of slaves was in question. And it had to be so, for acceptance of Africans as spiritual equals of whites would have brought up the whole uncom-

The Fripp House on St. Helena Island. Many plantation owners were appealed to by missionaries to hold a special service for slaves at least one Sunday each month. Some plantation owners often brought dozens of household slaves and field hands to Baptist services.

fortable subject of the morality of slavery. Though there had always been doubts gnawing away at white consciences, most felt trapped by custom and economic necessity to continue things as they were.

A cataclysmic event in 1739, however, changed a lot of minds, even if for the wrong reasons. A group of "Angola or Gullah Negroes," the Charleston papers reported, led by a conjureman, one "Gullah Jack," rose up in revolt at a plantation along the Stono River, a few miles south of the city. After killing their owner, his family, and several neighbors, they headed south for Spanish Florida where they hoped to find freedom among the Creek and Seminole Indians. The militia was called out, the offenders captured, jailed, and later executed.

The event predictably sent shockwaves through the white community, causing widespread panic. Even after the offenders were jailed and the immediate danger passed, questions remained. By this time, South Carolina was predominantly black, its 14,000 whites outnumbered nearly three to one. The colonial legislature immediately prohibited further importation of Africans, and Angolans already on the market found no buyers. When the ban was lifted, ten years later, the trade shifted back again to northwest Africa, to present-day Sierra Leone and Liberia.

A long-term solution was suggested in evangelism. It was thought that "Christian Negroes" would be more "tractable," less likely to revolt. After all, 14,000 whites could not

hope to keep nearly 40,000 Africans enslaved unless the Africans willingly submitted to slavery.

One of the wonderful things about Christianity was—and is—its utter subversiveness. Christianity was not Buddhism. It did not preach total acceptance of things as they are—or, in this case, as they were. Missionaries preached the angel's words to Hagar the slavegirl, ordering her to return to her mistress; the various Old Testament endorsements of slavery; and Paul's calls for obedience. But the slaves heard, "In Christ there is no slave, nor free,"—and the wonderful stories of the enslavement of the Jews, God's chosen people, first in Egypt, later in Babylon, and of their eventual liberation and restoration to their native land.

So slaves—spiritually cut off from native traditions and hungry for replacement—enthusiastically accepted Christ, not the ritualistic rich Anglican version, as might be expected, but the austere and enthusiastic Baptist faith, with its emphasis on charismatic conversion and total immersion. Since masters were loath to let slaves travel from plantation to plantation, even for Sunday worship, they allowed construction of chapels on each plantation—"praise houses," they came to be called. There slaves could gather and worship as they pleased, sometimes with a white preacher in attendance, but more often not. Black elders rose from among them, usually more gifted in exhortation than in traditional Christian theology.

Worship took on a distinctly African flavor, such as

Even after the Gullah got their own churches, they did not forget the days of the "praise house." Here, the Maryfield Plantation Praise House has been replicated on Daufuskie Island. The Gullah listened to preaching while sitting on rough pine benches, then rose to dance "the shout," a hymn of praise going back to tribal traditions.

"ring shouts," where the faithful danced in tight circles, working themselves into religious ecstasy while shouting. Hymn singing followed tribal "call and response" patterns where an elder, usually a sister with a strong voice, would sing out one line of an impromptu spiritual and the congregation would come back with the response. Such was a call for repentance: The sister would shout "Sheep, sheep, don't you know the road?" And the congregation would roar back "Yes, my Lord, I know the road!" Singing was always accompanied by enthusiastic hand clapping and foot stomping, often with drums and tambourines.

After emancipation, access to a cash economy allowed freedmen to build their first churches. The First Union African Baptist on Daufuskie Island dates from 1886.

Conservative white preachers were predictably horrified, thinking the slaves equated being devout with making noise. But those skeptical missionaries missed an important point. As ethnologist Margaret Washington Creel points out, "The Gullah's original interpretation of religion included viewing spirituality as a means of communal harmony, solidarity, and accountability. The fulcrum of the bondspeople's folk religion was spiritual and psychological autonomy."

And if Christianity unwittingly had set them free spiritually and psychologically, could political and economic freedom be far behind? That final freedom was a long time coming. But the yearnings were there from the very beginning.

Though most white slaveholders thought Gullah folk Christianity hardly worth comment, immediately after the Federal invasion of the sea islands, a folklorist commented on the "liberation theology" that had survived from the slave years. Laura Towne, Quaker schoolmarm who came to St. Helena Island in 1862 and stayed for nearly forty years, commented on the double meaning in Gullah hymns.

> Jesus make the blind see,
> Jesus make the cripple walk,
> Jesus make the deef to hear,
> Walk in, kind Jesus,
> No man can hinder we.

Though "we" in Gullah is often used for an all-purpose pronoun in place of "I," "me," or "us," in this hymn, at least, it has special meaning, referring to the Gullah people as a whole, a people who can neither be denied access to Jesus nor to freedom.

Another spiritual goes like this:

> I'm gonna mumble up ol' Zion
> In my heart, in my heart,
> Gonna mumble up ol' Zion
> In my heart.

Mumbling, of course, made the matter private. And yearnings of freedom must be kept so to avoid the wrath of master and the authorties, both so fearful of slave unrest because of the overwhelming numerical superiority of slaves.

Yet another beloved Gullah spiritual goes,

> The tallest tree in paradise,
> The Christian call the 'tree of life,'
> And I hope that trumpet call me home,
> To my New Jerusalem!

> Blow Gabriel!
> Trumpet blow louder, louder!
> And I hope that trumpet blow me home,
> To my New Jerusalem!

Paul and Silas bound in jail,
Sing God praise both night and day,
And I hope that trumpet blow me home,
To my New Jerusalem!

That "New Jerusalem," of course, was mentioned in Revelation, in the apocalyptic vision of John, when God would set the world right and "make all things new."

The Gullah Great Day of Jubilee came on November 7, 1861, a day still known in Gullah folklore as "When Gun Shoot." A powerful Union fleet shot its way into Port Royal Sound and put troops ashore on the outlying islands.

Local whites knew the end was coming. Word of the impending arrival of the Federal fleet had reached Beaufort during the middle of church services on Sunday, November 3. The rector of St. Helena's Episcopal, the town's most prestigious church, had interrupted his sermon and urged the faithful to abandon their homes and flee the approaching Yankee barbarians. A stampede followed, where nearly every white person in the county headed inland. Local legend says that only two remained. One was from New York and thought he did not have to leave. The other was so drunk he could not leave. Retreating planters set fire to cotton ready for shipment to Europe lest it fall into enemy hands, the flames lighting the night sky in all directions.

A few household slaves followed their masters and mistresses into exile. Most were left to their own devices. Many

slaves on outlying plantations, reasoning that war meant deliverance, headed for the sound of the cannonade. They descended upon baffled Federals in great clamoring hordes, seeking shelter and sustenance. One Yankee reported, "The Negroes were seen in great numbers, and, as the boats passed, came down to the shore with bundles in their hands, as if expecting to be taken off."

Within a few short weeks, the government had more slaves to feed than soldiers, sailors, and Marines. Maj. Gen. David Hunter set them all free in May of 1862 but, oddly enough, had his edict reversed by Abraham Lincoln. The slaves continued for nearly a year in legal limbo. Some were compelled to continue chopping and picking the cotton so badly needed by northern mills. Some were impressed into labor battalions and others into Black infantry units under white officers. But the most fortunate got land.

In 1863, Congress passed "An Act for Collection in the Insurgent Districts," which required plantation owners in the occupied areas of South Carolina to show up in person to pay their property taxes. This was impossible—intentionally—since by then most white males were either dead or in Confederate service. All the plantations went on the auction block. Though most went to Yankee speculators, some were subdivided and turned over to former slaves.

It was not the "forty acres and a mule" so widely promised and believed. The tracts ranged from ten to twenty-five acres, and mules were far too precious to give away. But

Lady's Island cabin, February 1892.
Courtesy of South Caroliniana Library, University of South Carolina, Columbia.

A mule was rarely part of the "forty acres and a mule" property redistribution program. Carts pulled by oxen became a preferred mode of transportation. Courtesy of South Caroliniana Library, University of South Carolina, Columbia.

many Gullah families received title to the land they and their ancestors had worked as slaves. This so-called "Port Royal Experiment" became the only egalitarian land redistribution in United States history. And the Gullah still hold onto much of that land, in spite of sporadic midnight workings of the Ku Klux Klan, the only slightly less murderous Redshirts, and the machinations of tax and real estate men in broad daylight.

The experiment was a success. The prophecy sung about in "New Jerusalem" had been fulfilled. Unlike the Children of Israel, the slaves had not been returned to their native land. They may have been in Babylon, but the land was theirs.

CHAPTER
THREE

The Power of the Root

Though it took western medicine a thousand years to realize the connection between a troubled mind and body sickness, the Gullah knew it from the beginning. And so, from the beginning, they saw no difference between faith and medicine. Jesus was "the great doctor," but so were the various medical doctors their masters retained to keep them healthy enough for work.

And there were other doctors as well—herbalist faith healers who plied a surreptitious trade in the slave quarters. Plantation owners generally tolerated these activities for two reasons. First, any attempt to suppress them may have led to unrest and dissatisfaction—and festering ill humor would have manifested itself in financial unprofitablity, at the very least. Second, mainstream medical practices in the late eigh-

teenth and early nineteenth centuries were, at best, largely ineffective and, at worst, more deadly than the maladies they attempted to cure. To be sure, a medical doctor could set a broken arm or leg, stitch up a gash, or apply salve to a skin ailment, but beyond that, he was essentially helpless. Peptic ulcers, tumors, hernias, and pinched nerves, led to years of degenerative misery; yellow fever, pneumonia, and cholera, to almost certain death.

Mosquito-borne illnesses were particularly dangerous, especially malaria, which seldom killed but left the sufferer in such poor condition he or she might succumb to other diseases that might otherwise not have been fatal. The South Carolina coast was a fertile breeding ground for mosquitoes. It would be many years before doctors would make the connection between malaria and the *anopheles* mosquito. Whites blamed the disease on swamp air. But many realized that malaria—or "swamp fever," as they often called it—was contracted during summer months. Accordingly, most plantation owners spent May through November either in town or in summer houses situated on high ground where they might catch sea breezes. One southerner remarked that he would sooner be shot at by a good rifleman than to spend one summer's night on his plantation.

This wholesale flight of whites for at least half of each year helped facilitate the survival of West African culture on the sea islands. Gullah slaves were left in the charge of a few overseers—some white, some black—who were indifferent to

the workings of herbalists and faith healers.

Many Gullah slaves noted that workings of a medical doctor might be as deadly as disease. Most camouflaged their ailments to avoid the purging, plastering, blistering, and blood-letting a doctor was sure to prescribe and saved their health complaints for the trusted herbalist.

Though the herbalist tradition had come over on the slave ships, the herbs had not. A few early slave herbalists picked up natural remedies from their contact with the last of the local Indians, but most gained their knowledge by empirical means: trial and error. Even so, they eventually gathered an extensive pharmacopoeia from field, swamp, and roadside plants. At first, the whites paid little attention, but when the Civil War blockade limited their access to imported drugs, they too turned to natural remedies. Francis Peyre Porcher, a Charleston physician and a surgeon in the Confederate Army, went to slave and Indian sources and identified over four hundred local plants with suspected medical value.

But the slave herbalist had another venue, one even less understood by whites: the realm of the spirit. Traditional African medicine taught that much sickness had its origins in spiritual evil, and drugs alone would not guarantee physical health. The spirit could have been sent by an enemy or could come of its own volition because of some lingering resentment from when it had been a living being. In either case, that spirit must be placated or exorcised.

Contents of a root doctor's "conjure bag."

This combination of spirit and medicine defies simple terminology. Nineteenth-century plantation journals refer to the practitioners as "slave doctors." The term hardly seems adequate. Its first mention in the press occurred in reports of the Stono Rebellion of 1739, when the uprising's leader was referred to as "Gullah Jack, a conjurer." That term, of course, neglects the herbal side of the practice. "Voodoo," from the Dahomean word "spirit," summons up the wild sexual overtones of rites practiced in New Orleans and Haiti. Folklorists have alternatively referred to the unique Gullah amalgamation of Christianity, herbalism, and magic

as "conjuration," "witchcraft," "hoodoo," or "rootwork." Contemporary practitioners, fearing both ridicule and "the long arm of the law," refuse to call themselves anything at all, simply saying "we help people." Root doctors and their root doctoring seem appropriate.

The law has been a persistent problem for root doctors. The tolerance of their work during slave times has vanished with the advance of modern medicine. Oddly enough, there is no law in South Carolina against the removing of spells, nor against the casting of them, even if such hexes result in disability or death. But if a root doctor gives a client a salve, a body oil, or any potion to be taken internally, he can be cited for "practicing medicine without a license," regardless of how benign the substance or effective the remedy might be. The famous Dr. Buzzard of St. Helena Island was fined and very nearly jailed for such indescretions. Dr. Bug of Laurel Bay Plantation was convicted of dispensing potions that gave young Gullah men heart flutters during their

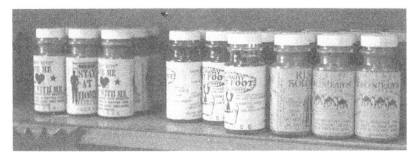

Neither root doctor nor store clerk will offer advice on the use of various potions and powders sold commercially.

World War II draft physicals.

Though retail outlets throughout the South offer such substances as "Love Balm," "Success Oil," and "Adam and Eve Herb," each carefully includes the word "alleged" on the label. And neither root doctor nor store clerk will offer any incriminating advice on their use. If a believer wants to purchase them and use them, that is fine, but he must do so on his own. The root doctor has retreated where the law will not, or cannot, go—into the world of spirit.

The root doctor's powers have been passed down the generations, from Africa to the present day. This transference of powers is called "passing the mantle." The mantle may be passed to a family member, usually a son, who is presumed to have inherited the clairvoyance necessary for a successful practice. Or it may be tendered to an apprentice who begins working for the conjureman by soliciting business or conveying customers to the site of conjuring, usually a remote location.

An interesting passing that occurred in neighboring Georgia in the 1920s is worthy of note. A man's hat blew off and another man retrieved it for him. Shortly thereafter, the first man died unexpectedly. Next, another man died suddenly after drinking from a well that had just been used by the hat retriever. The neighbors got to discussing the matter and concluded the man had "the death touch." Others refused to work with him and he was dismissed from his employment. Still others refused to rent him shel-

St. John the Conqueror is a popular root. When "dressed" with Hearts Cologne and prayer, the effect of the root allegedly is intensified as "High John the Conqueror." Roots vary with their intent, and while it may be difficult to get straightforward advice, a careful reading of the label can guide the amateur practitioner.

ter or even to serve him food. The man retreated to an is-land shanty and took up conjuring as a trade, simply be-cause there were no other options.

The root doctor probably got his name from the herbal origins of his practice. Indeed, the translated equivolent of "doctor" from the West African Fon and Twi languages means literally "observers of plants" and "workers with roots," respectively. But "the root" may not contain any herbs at all. The root is a charm—a mojo, a gris-gris, a hand—meant to be carried, worn, chewed, or buried, de-pending on its use and intent. Some are flannel packets, no bigger than a postage stamp, that contain powerful, often

secret ingredients. Others, particularly those meant to be buried, may be of wadded burlap, as large as a pecan or even a door knob, with protruding bones and feathers.

A particularly effective—and expensive—application of an evil root requires "chewing." The root doctor makes up a root, tracks down his victim and chews it in his presence, all the while making signs and speaking "unknown tongues." The effect is terrifying—the doctor swaying, muttering, eyes rolled back into his head, juice from the root running down his chin—and immediate, often bringing the victim to his knees.

Roots vary with their intent. Some are old standards: the "Follow Me" love charm, the "Money Root," the "John the Conker" (Conquerer)—when "dressed" with Hearts Cologne and prayer becomes the more powerful "High John the Conker," the "king of the root world"—and the dreaded

46

"Blue Root," widely reputed to cause wells and cows to dry up, chickens to cease laying, as well as sundry physical ailments, even death. Such roots may be kept in stock, but others are custom-made to a customer's unique situation and expectations.

Understandably, few root doctors will divulge their secrets. There are those, however, who believe the ingredients to be of secondary importance. The real power of a root, they claim, comes from magic words spoken in "unknown tongues" while the root is being prepared. While root doctors will not discuss the magic, they are willing to speak of ingredients. Typical ingredients of "good roots" may include herbs, asafedita, gunpowder, sulphur, salt, red or black candle wax, and various types of incense. "Bad roots" usually contain animal parts, crow feathers, salamander feet, a black cat's left thigh bone—more powerful if the cat has been burned alive. Both may include "goofer dust," graveyard dirt gathered just before midnight from the grave of a righteous Christian if the root is intended for good, or just after midnight from a heinous criminal's grave for evil workings. Special care must be taken not to offend graveyard spirits while gathering goofer dust. Though such spirits would probably be out making their rounds at midnight, it was commonly believed that one stayed behind as guard. One root doctor always left a shiny new dime on the grave in hopes the spirit would accept it as payment and not follow him home. Goofer, incidentally, is a corruption of the

Central African *kuwfa,* meaning a dead person.

Roots can bring success in business or love. They can cure physical and mental illness, protect a loved one, or slowly and painfully bring down an enemy. They can protect against spiritual visitation or bring the wrath of the hants down upon an offender.

If the case is not so serious as to warrant a root, the doctor may "mouth" the offender instead. Mouth is probably an abbreviation of "bad mouth," a term common in contemporary black speech, though today it connotes gossip and negativity rather than conjuration. Mouthing is similar to chewing the root, but without the root, and it need not be done in the victim's presence. It may bring bad luck, but not disaster; headaches and irritability, but not debilitating illness. Sheriff Ed McTeer was once threatened with a mouthing as an obstreperous young man. The effect, the conjurer claimed, would be thus: He would begin wetting his bed and his mother would whip him for it.

The "evil eye" is similar to mouthing, but must be administered in person—usually by a root doctor who casts a spell with malevolent looks, signs, and incantations in "unknown tongues." Its effects are similar, but generally more serious than mouthing. The evil eye can be cast along with an evil root, thus greatly aggravating the resulting ill effects.

Root doctors have other powers as well. They have been known to predict winning numbers in lotteries—both legal and clandestine, to control the roll of dice and the cut

of cards—and to sway judges and juries toward conviction or acquittal, as the client may direct.

Customers are generally obtained through referrals, much as in medical practice, since root doctors, ever afraid of legal entanglements, want only "the right people" among their clientele—the right people being believers who are able to pay and not likely to go running to the sheriff with a complaint. Like enlightened mental health counselors, most root doctors work on a sliding scale according to client income. That assessment is done informally, sometimes by merely noting the vehicle the client drives or the clothes he wears, by clairvoyance, or by a combination of these. New clients wisely avoid deception. Woe be unto the person who attempts to lie to a root doctor!

In whatever case, root doctors consider themselves professionals and charge accordingly. Unlike the legal profession, there is no free initial consultation. A tip on a winning number may cost as much as the lottery ticket. A love charm may run twenty-five dollars, depending on the desirability or coyness of the object of its intent. Untangling sticky family situations may cost five times that. And if there is a court case pending, the root doctor will charge as much as a skilled attorney.

The client is hardly in a position to negotiate a fee. First, he would not even be there were he not a believer. Second, root doctors command as much fear as respect. To risk annoying a root doctor over twenty, or even a hundred,

dollars would be foolish indeed.

A typical visit may go like this:

A man has terminated a relationship with a woman and taken up with another. His former lover dogs his trail, shows up at work, makes trouble with his employer. She calls his relatives and speaks ill of him, threatens to call the IRS over his failure to report casual income or the highway patrol with allegations of driving while intoxicated. He complains to a deputy sheriff who tells him to consult his attorney. He has no attorney, but finds one in the Yellow Pages and makes an appointment. The attorney outlines a number of vague but expensive legal options. He resorts to prayer but the results are inconclusive.

Finally, frustrated and desperate, disappointed by criminal and civil authority, too impatient for Divine intervention, he goes looking for Dr. Snake.

Dr. Snake does business in a backyard office at a remote island location. There are no signs to point the way, no name even upon the roadside mailbox. The client finds it by asking neighbors, whose helpfulness ranges from a profession of complete ignorance to vague directions. It takes him an hour to find it.

Once there, the man is ushered into a candlelit room, seated in a chair before the doctor's desk. The desk is cluttered with this and that—scraps of cloth, hardened pools of wax, mystical scribblings on bits of paper. There is African statuary in the corners, a large calendar with a picture of a

weeping Jesus upon the wall. Most Gullah see no conflict in the co-existence of Christianity and conjuration—both are true and good, and all good and true things come from God.

The doctor takes the man's left hand, feels between the metacarpals until he finds a strategic spot, then begins an interrogation.

"How long you two been together?"

"You-all got children?"

"You paying support?"

"How long you been apart?"

"You still sleeping with her?"

"Not even once in a while?"

The man feels the doctor's fingers working his hand bones, knows he is being read—as surely as if he were hooked to a polygraph—and the whole sordid truth comes rolling out in great torrents.

The doctor has seen it before, dozens, perhaps hundreds of times. He listens, finally pronounces, "She want you back."

It is not a question. The man nods his assent, then allows the woman has a peculiar way of showing affection.

"They all do," the doctor agrees. Then he adds, "This will be a tricky one."

The man nods again.

The doctor takes a pencil, writes a dollar amount on a piece of paper where the man can see it. This is a formal-

ity for the sake of the District Attorney, since the doctor has not actually asked for a fee.

The man looks at the amount, gulps. "You think you can help?" he asks.

The doctor looks into his eyes. "If I couldn't help people, you'd have never heard my name."

The man eagerly forks over the cash.

The doctor makes a notation in a journal, then asks more questions.

"What's her name?

The man tells him and the doctor writes it on a scrap of paper.

"How you spell yours?"

The doctor writes it down carefully on top of the woman's name. "Gimme a penny," he says.

The man hands it over. The doctor takes the coin and the paper, then retires to another room. The sound of clinking bottles, scraping, and soft muttering drifts through the wall. The man hears unintelligible words, then "Hag! Hag! Hag!"

The doctor comes back with the penny and the unknown added ingredients folded into the paper. "Wear this in your shoe," he says.

"Right or left?" the man asks.

"Left shoe. Give it to me."

The man unlaces his shoe, puts in on the desk. The doctor carefully places the root in the heel, hands the shoe

back. "Wear this for three days," he says, "then throw it in the river."

"Fresh water or salt?" the man asks, lacing his shoe, wanting to make sure no oversight of his own will impede the root's power.

"Don't matter. If it tears before three days, throw it in right away. I want to see it float."

The man takes note. The doctor did not say, "I want it to float" or "It needs to float." He used the word "see." By this time the man is absolutely sure that whatever river he finds himself near three days hence, the doctor will actually see the root being whisked away by the current.

The doctor gives further instructions. "Like I told you, this is a tough case. It may take a month, but in a few weeks you will notice a difference." Then the doctor reaches into a drawer, comes up with a twig. He breaks the twig into three pieces, wraps them in another scrap of paper. "If she comes around before then, pop one of these in your mouth and chew it."

The man opens the paper, looks dubiously at the pieces. "What is it?"

"Don't matter what it is. It won't hurt you. Just pop one in your mouth and chew."

The man folds the paper with the twigs into his wallet, then gets up to leave.

"You remember," the doctor says again, "three days."

The man nods his understanding. Already the root has

begun to throb and burn beneath his heel.

The doctor stops him as he reaches the door. "You call me in a month." He points at the calendar beneath the picture of Jesus. "Between 7:30 and 8:00, evening time."

The man leaves with the utmost confidence that his problem is on the mend. He has been given a "Shut Mouth" root, which works two ways. First, it makes him immune to further maligning. Second, it will stop the problem at its source. He will throw the root into the river at the appointed time, mention his visit to Dr. Snake to a confidant, a friend, perhaps a family member. But he will not say much about it. For, once cast, a root flies as true as a Zen arrow, needing no help from hand or tongue. And he will not dare to open the folded paper and try to discern why it misbehaves beneath his foot. Tampering with a root could cause it to backfire, making the problem worse instead of better.

And will the root actually help him? Probably so. If rootwork were not effective, the practice would have died out centuries ago. Most likely, one of the man's confidants will mention the conjuration to another, and the news will go whispering through the community until the rejected woman hears that she has been rooted. And since she knows in her heart that all her subversion was wrong in the first place, she will immediately desist her sundry annoyances.

But there is another disconcerting possibility. The

woman has already shown herself to be troublesome and perseverent. She may have saved a scrap of her former lover's clothes, perhaps a snip of hair, a piece of toenail or fingernail. With this, she has the option of retaining her own root doctor and requesting a "Follow Me" root to try and get her man back. Then a full-scale spiritual warfare will commence, with further visits to conjuremen, the casting of more roots, maybe even spells and hexes flying back and forth.

Thus, this aspect of root doctoring fills a niche roughly equivalent to litigation in the majority culture. A white suburbanite has papers served on him by a neighbor over some trifling offense—the location of a property line, a driveway, or perhaps an annoying dog knocking down a child. The suburbanite retains his own attorney, fills out affidavits, pays various filing fees, and the papers go flying back and forth via the U.S. Postal Service or process servers. The original litigant responds in kind and the conflict escalates, each new arrival of papers bringing dread and each subsequent legal consultation bringing a strange sense of comfort and satisfaction.

Ignoring such legal proceeding could result in judgement by default, the seizure of property or the garnishment of funds. But remaining heedless of spiritual warnings could have even more dire consequences. Charleston author DuBose Heyward, best known for his collaboration with George Gershwin to produce *Porgy and Bess*, relates such a

tale of haunting in his short story *The Half Pint Flask,* wherein a man is driven to madness and attempts suicide after he removes an ornament from a Gullah grave.

Another less literary incident is related by this author's father, Roger Pinckney, Sr., who served as coroner of Beaufort County for thirty-six years. The coroner was called out to investigate violent or mysterious deaths. Even with the grisly parade of shootings, knifings, drownings, and auto wrecks, it was still only a part-time position. The rest of the time, he built docks, seawalls, and bridges on creeks, rivers, and estuaries. He recalls an incident where marine construction and mysterious death coincided:

It was about 1966, I believe, and I got a call from this doctor in Savannah. He said, "Coroner, I got this Beaufort man over here and he died."

And I said, "Did he die in Beaufort County?"

And he said, "No, he died in Savannah."

And I said, "Then what's that got to do with me?"

He said, "I need some help with the paperwork."

I told him I'd try.

So he said, "I thought he had cancer. He wouldn't eat, couldn't sleep, was just wasting away. He was a veteran, so I sent him to Augusta for tests. He was up there two weeks. They all came

back negative. They couldn't find anything wrong with him. Just before he died, he said that I could not help him, that no doctor could. He said he had been rooted."

And so I said, "Where's he from?"

And he said, "Daufuskie Island."

And I said, "Hell, I remember him! I was working on a dock there and this man came running out of the woods saying, 'Come quick. These two men are fighting in the beer joint.' And I told him I didn't care if they fought. But he wouldn't listen. 'Come quick,' he says. 'They gonna kill each other.' And I told him, 'I'm the coroner. If one of them kills the other, then I'll come.'

"Pretty soon, this black man comes running down the bank, like all hell was after him. He jumps into a boat and rows out into the river. After a bit, another black man runs out of the woods, out onto the dock. He yells, 'You may have got away this time, you son of a bitch, but I'll fix you! I'm gonna root you!'"

There was this long silence on the other end of the line. Finally I said, "Doctor, you're not from around here, are you?"

And he says, "No, I'm from New Jersey."

Then there was another long silence, so I said, "Well, what can I help you with?"

And he says, "Coroner, what should I put on the death certificate?"

So I told him, "You write DIED OF UNDE-TERMINED NATURAL CAUSES. I know the coroner over there in Savannah, and that'll be just fine with him."

Root throwing may have international implications. After the arrest and incarceration of Dr. Bug for helping Gullah draftees fail their physicals for induction into the military, dozens, perhaps hundreds, of young men went to root doctors in an effort to foreshorten World War II before their inductions. It is commonly believed the atomic bomb was the result. And it has also been theorized, the mysterious and elusive "Gulf War Syndrome" is the result of a massive hexing performed by Saddam Hussein.

CHAPTER FOUR

A Familiarity with Spirits

Chalmers S. Murray, writing of Gullah beliefs on his native Edisto Island, remarked, "A ghost means about the same thing to a Negro as it does to a white man—the materialized body of one who is dead. But no white man has ever claimed to know as much about a ghost's habits as does a sea island black."

Murray's peer, Dr. Chapman J. Milling, a physician and psychologist at the South Carolina State Hospital for thirty years, was no stranger to the affliction of roots and spirits. Milling recalls the words of a tormented Gullah patient: "A hant is as natural as a man with britches."

This familiarity with spirits has its origins in Africa, where many tribes practiced the ritual of the second burial. Because a corpse decomposes quickly in the tropical heat,

the initial burial took place within a day or two of death. The time was too short for a gathering of the dead person's relatives or for adequate rituals. A year or two later, the relatives were summoned for a great feast, the bones were exhumed, carefully wrapped in leaves or cloth, and prayerfully and lovingly put in their final resting place. No property could be transferred until the second burial, and until this time the spirit could not rest easy.

But once in America, plantation masters did not give their slaves the luxury of two funerals—burials took place quickly, often at night by torchlight, so as not to take valuable time away from fieldwork. And the exhuming of a body was one African ritual Christian elders would not tolerate. So, spirits were condemned to suffer an eternity of

Beaufort County's intense spiritual activity may have origins in its violent past. Even unbelievers shudder when gazing upon careening gravestones and ghostly ruins, such as Old Sheldon Church, twice destroyed—by the British during the Revolution and by General Sherman during the Civil War.

Even true believers shudder when looking upon the ruins of the old plantations.

unrest, becoming, in the Gullah lexicon, "trabblin' spirits."

And the living would bear the consequences.

Another factor in the considerable spiritual activity encountered by the Gullah was the violent history of their new home. Since 1562, when the first white men set foot in what was to become Beaufort County, time has woven a nearly continuous tapestry of violence and destruction. Over the centuries, battle, murder, and sudden death have cut deep into the ranks of six nations. The French came first. They were starved into cannibalism. The English threw the diners into the Tower of London. And the Spanish butchered the rest over theological, rather than gastronomical, differences. English and Scots threatened the Spanish, then each other. Yemassee Indians, withering under European disease and thievery, tomahawked the palefaces whenever the opportunity arose. Americans fought the English twice, then fired a great fratricidal holocaust over slavery and southern independence. Meanwhile, hurricanes, fires,

This shanty, which still stands on Coosaw Island, is painted in traditional Gullah fashion. The blue door, blue windowframes, and pillars are painted with the intention of keeping the plentiful spirits at bay.

and epidemics, heedless of nationality or creed, added to the ranks of the dead. If tortured life and violent death give rise to restless spirits, the Gullah home on the sea islands should be the ghost capitol of America. Indeed, even unbelievers shudder when looking upon the ruins of old plantations, ancient graveyards with headstones careening this way and that, mournful giant oaks dripping with long gray strings of Spanish moss, as tidal rivers murmur long forgotten secrets.

Some of these spirits would never harm a person, other than scaring him to death. But they might make a person harm himself.

Gullah riverman Dan Williams refused his boss's suggestion that he serve as night watchman on a heavy laden barge.

"What's the matter, Dan?" his boss chided. "You ain't afeared of ghost?"

"No sir!" Dan answered, emphatically.

"Then why won't you watch the load tonight?"

"Well, Cap," Dan replied, "ghost ain't gone hurt you. You is gone hurt yourself gettin' out the way!"

Prior to the Revolution, when coastal plantations produced indigo dye for English cloth, planters gave their slaves the dregs from the boiling pots, which the slaves used to decorate window frames and porch posts, in the belief the blue color kept the plentiful spirits at bay. When indigo cultivation declined in the 1780s, Gullah slaves continued the

custom with blue paint. It is a practice that survives to this day, perhaps no longer for a spiritual repellent but as a tradition.

Another surviving tradition is the passing of young children over the grave. If a parent or grandparent were to suffer a painful or untimely death, it was commonly believed the mourning spirit would return to visit the children it loved during its lifetime. The children would be restless, fretful, unable to sleep. Health problems would inevitably result. The spirit could be placated during a graveside service by passing all young children in the family back and forth over the coffin. It continues to be a tradition in many Gullah funerals.

Grave decorations were another way to quiet restless spirits. In a tradition still practiced in central Africa, the last articles used by the deceased were placed upon the grave, in the belief they bore a strong spiritual imprint. Bottles, pots, and pans were common. In later years they were augmented by unused medicines, eye glasses, telephones, toasters, electric mixers, even sewing machines and televisions.

Remains of ritual found on grave near Sheldon, South Carolina. (See pages 66–67 for diagram.) Photographs courtesy of Sea Island Historic Society.

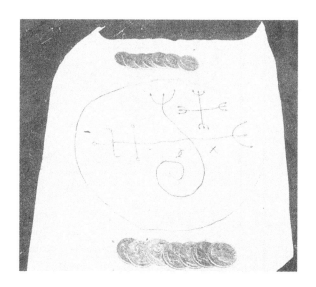

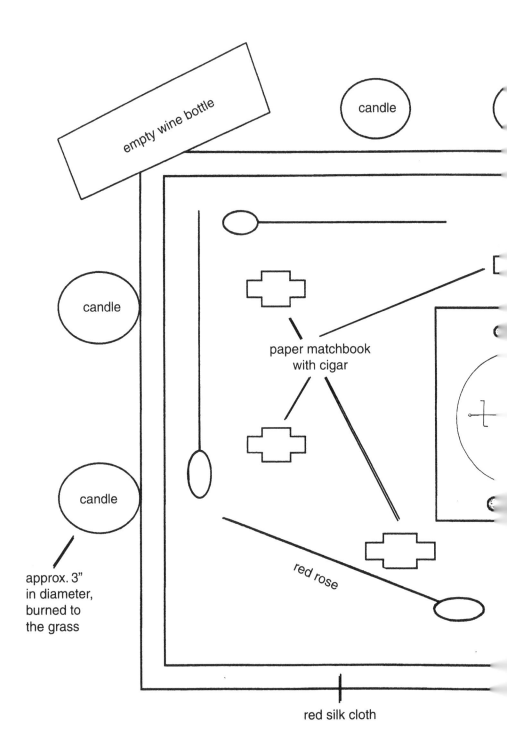

empty wine bottle

candle

candle

candle

paper matchbook
with cigar

red rose

approx. 3"
in diameter,
burned to
the grass

red silk cloth

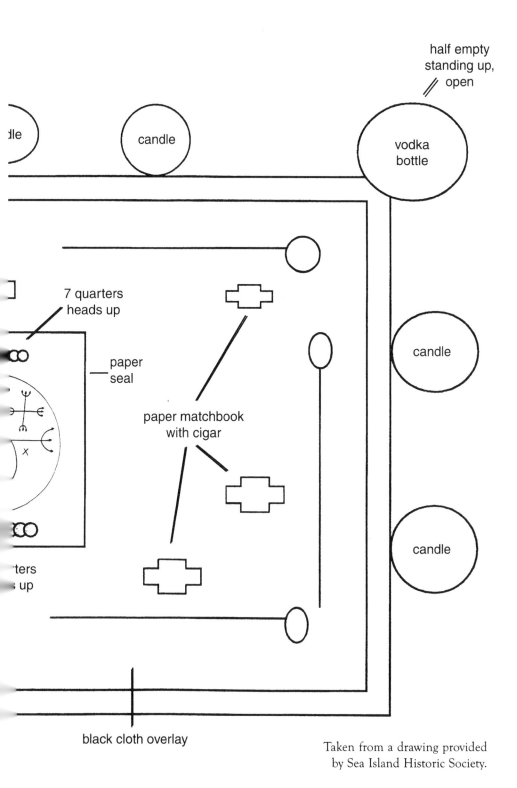

half empty
standing up,
open

candle

candle

vodka
bottle

7 quarters
heads up

paper
seal

paper matchbook
with cigar

candle

candle

ters
up

black cloth overlay

Taken from a drawing provided
by Sea Island Historic Society.

The articles are broken before placement on the grave. Prior to full realization of the African connection, observers theorized the objects were rendered useless to prevent theft. Now it is believed the breaking was ritual, symbolizing the end of things in this world.

Many graves were surrounded by rows of conch shells, arranged like a fence to keep the spirit in. The practice is widespread in Africa, as well as across Black America. Andre Pierre, Haitian artist and voodoo priest says, ". . . shells symbolize the existence of the spirit in the sea. . . . The shell encloses elements of earth, water, and wind . . . the world in miniature." When a curious folklorist asked an elderly Gullah sister the significance of the shells, the sister replied considerably more succinctly, "The water brought us, the water will take us home." It was a simple but heavy metaphor symbolizing the unique merging of African and Christian belief in Gullah spirituality: The slave ships had brought them to America, and they would eventually cross the River Jordan to their heavenly home.

The root doctor was yet another protector against unwanted visitation. He could prescribe numerous remedies, including prayers, roots, incense, and powder that was sprinkled around the yard, across the doorsteps, or around the bed. The root doctor, however, had other spirits at his command, spirits that had never had bodies and had always existed in the shadow world, spirits he could unleash to do evil if directed to do so by an enemy. Thus, the root doc-

tor was not only protection, but danger as well—a man surely not to be trifled with.

The observation made by Chalmers Murray about the similarity of Gullah and white belief is only partially correct. Some spirits are indeed beings who are released from human bodies upon death. But others are inhabitants of a parallel spiritual universe who cross over into the material world at will or by command. Yet others alternate between spirit and flesh. Like viruses, forever shifting between a life form and a chemical equation, these spirits torment by midnight, but at noon benignly go about their business, innocently shopping, cooking, weeding the backyard garden, with perhaps no more than a wicked grin denoting their true intent.

The "hag" is particularly troublesome. To begin with, there are two types: the hag that is total spirit, the "hag hag," and the "slip-skin hag," which is a person, usually a female, who becomes invisible by shedding her skin—pulling it over her head like a sweater—and going out to wreak havoc after dark. Both types gain entry into a house through a chimney or keyhole, then ride the afflicted person in his sleep.

"You can't speak when they gets on you," a hagged man testified. "You might think you're hollering but you ain't. They rides you night after night, till you get so poor you can't hardly live."

Like the *incubus* in European folklore, one of the hag's

more insidious habits is to use a man sexually in his sleep. If the hag is the standard variety and becomes overly fond of its host, it is likely to remain on the premises during daylight hours, so anything on which the hag might "roost"— bedposts, coat hooks, a floor lamp—must be removed. A root doctor may be retained for powders or incense. Or if the person possesses a strong enough will, he may wrest himself from sleep and attempt to lay hands on the offending spirit. "You can't see 'em, but they feel like a piece of raw meat," one man said. "And you can't catch 'em neither. But if you get your hand on 'em, even for a second, you can scare 'em so they won't come back."

A slip-skin hag is another matter entirely. These arrive after dark and leave before *dayclean*, and thus may be intercepted at the point of entry. Hags apparently have a great fondness for mathematics, but are not very good at it. A common hag repellent is a colander or a sifter hung over the doorknob. Though a hag can easily slip through either, it will generally stop to count the holes. Before it can get too far, however, it will lose count and have to start over. This wastes valuable time and before long, "dayclean catch 'em" and it must return to its daylight occupation.

Salt is another common remedy. It may be sprinkled around the bed in hopes the hag may shed her skin at bedside, with predictable results when she attempts to slip back inside. If the hag slips her skin before making her rounds, it must be located and salted in anticipation of her daylight

return. Such an incident is reported to have occurred in Charleston in 1916. Neighbors suspected a certain woman of going out after dark and tormenting a former lover who had found a new partner. They found the skin hanging behind the woman's bedroom door, salted it thoroughly, and waited anxiously in the closet. The woman came in at dawn and commanded the skin back into its rightful place. The skin, in salty misery, did not respond. "Skin, skin, don't you know me?" the woman pleaded. The neighbors leapt from the closet and the hag disappeared into thin air, never to return.

Hags also hate publicity. If a person suspects visitation and also suspects the hag's identity, he can write the person's name and "hag" over his front door. If he is correct, the hag will be deterred from entering.

A more direct, but legally risky, approach is direct confrontation. Schoolteacher Laura Towne reported the severe beating of a woman by an afflicted neighbor. The man apologized to Miss Towne the following morning, but claimed he had no choice, since the woman had hagged him. He steadfastly refused an apology to the woman he had assaulted, but said it probably would not happen again, since the hagging would no doubt stop. Miss Towne did not record any further trouble between either party—on physical or spiritual planes.

Lacking a human to ride, hags will sometimes take to horses. If a farmer hears his horses neighing and kicking in

their stalls at night and finds them lathered up in the morning, he might blame hags for the trouble. If he finds manes worked into strange little knots—hag stirrups—he can be quite sure of it.

If a hag on its spectral rounds chooses to carry a lantern, it becomes a "Jack Mullater," a "Jack-o-Lantern," or a "ghost light." The hag has someplace to go and a limited amount of time to get there and back, so a Jack Mullater rarely stops to threaten nighttime travelers. But a hag can go where a man on horse or afoot cannot, effortlessly cruising three to five feet above the ground. Any attempt to follow a Jack Mullater, however, would likely bring disaster. To throw its pursuer off the trail, the hag will take off through the swamp, where the follower might mire and drown.

Oddly enough, this Jack Mullater is the only being in the Gullah spirit world that yields to scientific scrutiny. There are high concentrations of natural phosphorescence in island swamps—rotten stumps, clumps of dirt, leaves, even mushrooms, will glow at night with an eerie luminescence. Under the right conditions—often a particularly still and sultry night—the phosphorous collects in concentrations the size of a muskmelon and drifts through the swamps. If there is a road nearby, its surface, still warm from the day's intense sunlight, draws cooler air from the swamps, the Jack Mullater along with it.

Such a phenomenon regularly occurs on Lands End Road on St. Helena Island, where dozens often gather to

watch the ghostly spectacle. Some whites say it is the ghostly headlight from a migrant labor bus that hit a roadside oak years ago with fatal results. Others claim it is an unfortunate Confederate artilleryman who was decapitated by a Yankee cannonball. But the Gullah know it is a hag on its way to make mischief.

The Gullah have also been plagued by a number of spirit animals. Some look normal enough but will raise goosebumps as they cross your trail. They also emit an odor of raw meat and walk with a particular high-stepping gait. "Conjure-horses" and "spirit-bears" used to be common but inexplicably vanished in the years immediately following the Civil War. Both were larger than their physical counterparts, breathed fire, and tormented late night travelers, often following for miles at treetop height, roaring like wind and booming like thunder.

"Boogers" looked like alligators, but they would vanish in a flash of light upon recitation of the Lord's Prayer. Chapman Milling reported Crummie Harrison's encounter with such a booger while crossing the Wateree Swamp after a church prayer meeting in 1936.

> The thing lay motionless in the road. At first, Crummie thought it was a 'gator, and since it showed no intention of moving, he turned toward an alternate route. Farther on, he encountered the thing again. This time he saw the thing had twice

the usual number of legs–four on each side–and what he believed was smoke coming from its mouth and eyes "as big as ox eyes" that glowed like dying coals. But Crummie was still full of prayer meeting spirit and a "good Christian man," as he described himself. He was not going to let a "debilish critter" win a dispute over the use of a public road and "run his pants off in the briars." He drew his pistol and fired six times into its body. In a flash the booger was gone. When Crummie got to the spot, he found ashes and cinders, "just like a man had built a fire and the rain had outened it."

But perhaps the most dreaded spirit was the "plateye." In the old days, pirates such as Blackbeard, Bluebeard, and Stede Bonnet preyed on Spanish galleons, then put ashore in Carolina to bury their booty. Typically, the pirate captain would summarily execute the men who did the burying, so he alone would know the treasure's location. Then he would throw the bodies atop the chest and cover them up. Some believe these dead sailors became plateyes and would rise from the spot to chase away interlopers. Some say they would assume the forms of animals, usually a six-legged calf or a headless hog.

Others believe plateyes are permanent residents of the spirit world, coming into ours to work retribution against

wrongdoers or do mischief at a root doctor's command. One of the most disconcerting habits of the plateye is his ability to change forms appropriate to individual occasions. A man who murdered his wife on Coosaw Island was reportedly lured to his death in Lucy Point Creek by a plateye who came to him in the form of his dead wife. A St. Helena man whose daughter died after a lingering illness—he believed, because he had neglected to seek the assistance of a root doctor—was visited by her spirit who "would drift right through the wall and set there in her leettle chair." Because the apparition refused to speak or acknowledge her father, the man assumed it was a plateye tormenting him. And it was a plateye in taking the form of a former lover that nearly drove an offender to suicide in Heyward's "The Half Pint Flask."

Exorcising a plateye might prove especially difficult, since the spirit plays on a person's guilt. In "The Half Pint Flask," the plateye was placated when the offender replaced the purloined grave ornament. In the case of murder, or some other irreversible crime, such placation is impossible, and the plateye usually has its way. The plateye has a great weakness, however: it is quite fond of whiskey. Thus the wise traveler carries a flask with him. If a plateye gives chase, he can pour a little whiskey on the ground, and the spirit will stop to lap it up, allowing an escape to safer territory.

Such whiskey drinking by spirits also turns up in one of Milling's stories about a late night 'coon hunt in the

swamp. The hounds—Clinch, Barker, Mike, and Woman— usually afraid of nothing, began growling and cowering at the hunters' feet. Milling's companion, one Demus Newton, was certain the dogs smelled a "hant." Milling had a nose as good as any hound's, but for a story rather than 'coon. After much encouragement, Demus told of a previous en- counter, when his dogs sensed another spirit.

Jerry Isaacs was old Sam Isaac's brother. Sam died long befo' my time, but this here Jerry was around my Pa's age, I reckon. He was always a wicked man, could cuss worse and drink mo' than anybody else. Truth is, liquor was his ruination. When he got ol', he got so mean, no woman would live with 'em, or have nothing to do with 'em. He stay in a log house, the other side of this here slough, and all he do was hunt and trap. He catch enough 'coon to pay for the ration he need, and the liquor too. And he spend three time on the li- quor what he do on the food. Every Sat'day he go to Jeems' sto' an buy little-bitty rations, then take out for ol' Kiah Johnson still. An' from Sat'day night till Monday mornin', he be lyin' right in the middle of the shanty flo', drunk and glad of it.

One Sat'day, jus' about a year gone, I go to the sto' to buy my week ration, an' Ol' Man Jeems say to me, "Demus, wherebouts is ol' Jerry Isaacs? He

ain't been here this evenin'." So I tell 'em I speck he got hold of liquor befo' he got to the sto' and ain't nobody gone see 'em till next week. Ol' Man Jeems he laugh an' say Jerry could be laying there dead an' nobody would know it till the buzzards fin' 'em.

Well, long 'bout dusk-dark, I get my rations an' start fo' home, but befo' I gets there, I take a notion to go 'coon huntin'. I got to the house an' tell Katie I gone to the swamp. I get these same dogs here, an' I get me a little liquor too. I ain't drink much, just enough to make me kinda spry an' help me along, an' a little mo' in case a moccasin snag me.

I stop by Crummie to ax him to go, but he gone to the sto'. Then I stop by Phillip Lijah's an' holler for him to go. But he say his wife kinda puny, an' he better stay home.

Now, I don't like goin' in the swamp by myself, 'cause of snake an' thing, but I was mighty nigh there by now, an' the dogs struck up a sassy trail. I follow 'em an' pretty soon I in the middle of the swamp. Ol' Woman she treed, and when I got there, I shine my light up in the cypress tree an' there is the bigges' 'coon I ever see. Well, I didn't have no gun, so I taken my axe an' begin a choppin'. The dogs was a goin' wild, gnawin' and bitin' at them chips, when pretty soon, Ol' Woman

commence to growl, way down in she throat, an' all the dogs back off in the dark. I look 'round an here ol' Jerry Isaacs, a standin' there with empty fruit jar in both he hand.

"Hey Unka Jerry," I hollers. "You sho' scared me. Way them dogs was actin', I was sure they smelt a hant. Wanta help me get this 'coon?"

"What you talking 'bout, boy?" he says. "Ain't no 'coon up that tree!"

I look up the cypress an' sho' nuff, that 'coon gone. I never see 'em jump an' there ain't no place he could a gone.

Unka Jerry was standin' there in the path an' he look at me an' say, "How 'bout a drink a that liquor you got there, son?"

How in the name o' sense he know I got any liquor be beyon' me, but he look like he need a drink real bad, so I han' him the bottle. He take 'em an' turn 'em up to he mouth an' when he get through, there ain't nary a drap lef'. Then he laugh an' throw the bottle way off in the woods an' say to me, "I thank you, son. I ain't had a drink since last Sat'day an' here it is Sat'day again. That sho' was good. That the best liquor I ever drink."

When he say that I hears a yelp and the dogs come runnin' back to me, with they tails betwixt they legs. On they go, right out of the swamp, so

I know I ain't gone get no 'coon tonight. So I says to Unka Jerry, "Well, I glad to seen you, 'cause Ol' Man Jeems was axing 'bout you this evenin'. I reckon I'll see you at the sto' nex' Sat'day."

But Unka Jerry ain't answer. Is you recken when I look 'round do I see ol Unka Jerry? No sir! He gone! Gone jus' the way that 'coon were gone!

Well, I didn't waste no time gettin' home, an' I mighty glad when I get there too. The dogs beat me an was whinin' at the do' when I reach the step. I never been so glad to get my foot to my own fire.

An when next mornin' come, you reckon what happen? Jus' fo' church, Phillip Lijuh come by in he buggy and holler out to me an Katie 'bout ol Jerry Isaacs done been dead. I say, "He can't be dead, cause I jus' see 'em in the swamp las' night."

He say, "Shut yo' mouth, boy! That man been dead lease a week! Ol' Man Jeems was gettin' uneasy 'bout 'em an' send the Wilson boys afer 'em. They fine 'em dead in bed with two liquor bottles by him. Them boys so scared they ran all the way to Doc Jackson. Doc Jackson check 'em an say he done been dead since 'bout las' Sat'day."

It hard to say how I feel when Phillip Lijuh say them words. I knowed right then I done hol' compersation with a hant, and he drunk up all my whiskey.

CHAPTER FIVE

Remedies, Cures,
Bad Luck and Good

Not all preventive medicine was the sole property of the root doctor. Many herbal remedies were known to laypersons and widely administered and believed. Many are difficult to duplicate, since folk healers never used scientific names for herbal ingredients. So a word of caution: Some ingredients that are commonly mentioned in Gullah herbospiritual folklore—cocklebur, jimson weed, and dogwood—are well known, but others like silk root, blacksnake root, shoestring root, and rattlesnake master necessitate a field collaboration between a trained botanist and a Gullah herbalist for positive identification. Unfortunately, such an exhaustive study has yet to be made.

This is another compelling irony in Gullah history: While tens of thousands rally to protect the Brazilian rain forest from clear-cutting because of the assumed loss of yet-to-be-discovered cures, a vast pharmacopeia—already discovered, but underdocumented and nearly lost in humankind's rush to "progress"—lies right beneath our noses. An African proverb attests, "Each time an elder dies, a library closes." And most of the Gullah herbalists have "crossed the water" again and are no longer with us. If Dr. Bug could cause heart flutters sufficient to cause dozens of young men to fail their draft physicals—and send Dr. Bug to jail—what may be assumed of the "Adam and Eve plant" that was known to calm a restless, and love tortured, breast? Is the Adam and Eve plant, *Apelectrum hyemale,* a member of the orchid family, as some have assumed, or is it something else entirely? Bull nettle, maybe *Solanum carolense,* was a reputed cure for epilepsy. A mysterious blue-white mushroom, perhaps *Psylicibe cubensis,* grows naturally upon piles of manure left by Gullah cows and ponies. What wild secrets wait to be discovered there?

Some common—and proven—herbal remedies include the following: green cockleburs made into a poultice for skin ailments; ginger root tea for stopped or irregular menses; regular baths in a mixture of teas from dogwood roots, cherry roots, and oak bark for muscular swelling; cockroach tea for persistent coughing; and earthworm tea mixed with lard as a good salve for rashes, as well as

bloodroot tea. A dash of peppermint oil will ease stomach pains in adults, and chamomile tea sweetened with honey will calm the most colicky infant. The leaves from cassena, a holly-like shrub common on the sea islands, contain a powerful stimulant and may be substituted for coffee or tea. Basil leaves in the bath make a natural deodorant and also might offer protection from hexing. Dog fennel root tea is a general invigorant. Difficulty in urinating may be cured with diluted wild grapevine sap. Persimmon sapwood and maple bark teas reputedly ease cataracts.

Other remedies remain more obscure, some because no research has ever been done on what may seem a positive cure, others because of the difficulty in positively identifying the necessary ingredients. As an example of the former, the

In the 1980s Charleston's best root supply store looked like any other pharmacy.

Gullah widely use turpentine as an emergency balm, antibiotic, and sealant for cuts, abrasions, and lacerations while working in the pinewoods. Gunpowder mixed with whiskey will "calm the heart and give power." Benefits from turpentine and whiskey may be enthusiastically debated with less than certain conclusions, but smokeless gunpowder contains nitroglycerine, a common heart stimulant.

Examples of the latter, less-than-positively identified ingredients, are many. Alligator root is a sedative. Bitterweed, an herb that makes cows give bad-tasting milk, will cure chills. Blackroot will cause violent vomiting in the case of inadvertent poisoning. Ashes from brambleberry sticks mixed with bluestone and alum, chewed and spit on sores, will bring immediate relief. A wash of the roots of the heartleaf plant will clear up bloodshot eyes and clear the vision.

Complaints that have origin in the spiritual plane may require more drastic treatments. One hexed Charleston woman was having fits that made her crawl around on the floor, barking and howling like a dog. She was cured by a root doctor who made two conjure bags of ground rattle-snake rattles and bade her wear them in her armpits. A woman south of Little River, South Carolina, took to walking around naked and mooing like a cow after an enemy fixed her by putting a potion in her fish supper. She was cured, interestingly enough, by a concoction called "Bull of the Woods," a tea from *Similia similibus curantor,* that made

her vomit grass.

A St. Helena Island child suffering from asthma was treated thusly: On the advice of a root doctor, her mother took a hank of hair from her head, took her outside and stood her beside a willow tree. The mother drilled a hole into the willow, even with the top of the girl's head, inserted the hair into the hole, plugged it with a willow twig. Both girl and willow grew, but the girl faster. When the girl surpassed the plugged hole, the asthma disappeared.

A man was hexed into slobbering fits. He would sit in his chair all day, whip his head from side to side, slinging saliva on himself, his clothes, the table, even the wall. A root doctor took hair from the tail of a horse, soaked it in corn whiskey, and washed out the man's eyes. The fits vanished immediately.

And the stories continue.

A man jilted a girl, but she had taken hair from his head and had a root prepared in a bottle that she buried beneath his steps. Every time the man passed over the root, he suffered convulsions, many accompanied by a violent grinding of his teeth. His neighbors inserted stones into his mouth to save his teeth, and the man chewed them up and spat them out. The convulsions became more frequent and more violent, occurring even when the man did not pass over the root. His neighbors and friends had to physically restrain him by tying him into his bed. Three medical doctors gave diagnoses ranging from tuberculosis to hyperten-

sion and medicated him accordingly. Nothing helped. Plans were made for a funeral. Finally, a female root doctor prescribed nine ritual baths in a mixture of water, salt, and baking soda, followed by a dose of iodine and potash and a rub-down with olive oil. It worked. The man, once given up for dead, recovered completely, married another woman, and raised a family.

A salve of lard rendered from a buzzard's carcass will ease stiffness in the legs, especially if the problem is caused by walking over an evil root buried beneath the doorstep. The odor is hard to take, but the results are well worth it. Buzzard grease must be used sparingly, or a person will get so limber, he can no longer walk. The feathers can be burned, then mixed with vinegar to form a paste. Plastered around the front doorframe, this paste will repel the person who buried the evil root, in case he should come back to do more mischief.

The buzzard can also provide a powerful talisman—for the person brave enough to obtain it. A seeker must wait until the female buzzard leaves her nest to feed, then he must climb up and steal an egg. This is no mean feat, since the buzzard, like the eagle and the osprey, only nests in remote and extremely precarious locations, perhaps in a lightning blasted pine, fifty or sixty feet or more from the ground. If the seeker survives the climb and descent, he then boils the egg to kill the embryo, waits until the buzzard leaves again, replaces it. The buzzard apparently is a

diligent incubator. When the boiled egg refuses to hatch, the buzzard frets over it for days, finally performs a test. The buzzard takes a rock, or a bit of oyster shell, and attempts to break the egg and liberate the chick. When it finally gives up, the seeker climbs the tree again and retrieves the object the buzzard used to crack the shell. Understandably, the resulting buzzard-test rock is believed to have great power, protecting the owner from all evil. In the 1930s such rocks were greatly prized by burglars in Charleston and New Orleans, perhaps other places as well, since it was thought to make them invisible after dark.

Commercial lye, especially Red Devil brand, was a common spiritual cleansing agent. If a woman suspected an enemy had rooted her by sprinkling some evil on her steps or porch, a thorough dusting and scrubbing with Red Devil might bring relief. Likewise, an unopened can buried beneath the gate, "as deep as your elbow," will keep evil out of the yard. The effect is amplified if nine ten-penny nails and nine new straight pins are buried along with the lye.

Graveyard dirt—the goofer dust in roots—may be applied by a layperson to minimize spiritual visitation or to cure a variety of day-to-day problems. The dirt should be gathered at midnight from the spot on the grave just above the corpse's heart. The gatherer should choose a person he or she knows—ideally, one who has not been dead for more than three or four years. Like in dirt gathered for rootwork, the personality of the departed is important: a godly man

for good, a bad man for evil, a successful businessman for financial acumen, a gambler for luck with cards or dice. Money must be left at the gravesite and prayers to the dead must be spoken—though in the case of a ritual at an evil person's grave, a good cursing will suffice instead.

The gatherer can assume a familiarity with the spirit, and begin his monologue with such invocations as, "You remember me when you was alive. You never had no trouble with me, and I'm asking you to help me now. . . ." The petitioner then gets specific with his or her request. If the spell is intended for evil, the petitioner might add, "You was always a no good son of a bitch, raising hell to make things go your way. Now, make things go my way. . . ."

Once gathered, graveyard dirt should be nourished so the spirit dwelling therein will not lose power. Sulphur, saltpeter, salt, or sugar are said to work equally well to keep the spirit active. Graveyard dirt may be spread around one's property to repel evil. Others sprinkle it in their shoes, so they may walk on evil without picking it up.

Picking up evil by walking on it was common. Evil, being spiritual, is everlasting. It can be foiled, driven off, or displaced, but never destroyed. Exorcise a spirit from a person or place, and that spirit will have to find another home, usually in some unfortunate person who is just walking along, minding his own business, when he is struck down. Though this belief is inherent in West African religion, there is a Biblical parallel in the eighth chapter of the book

of Matthew, when Jesus drives devils from a man into a herd of pigs, which subsequently rush into the sea and drown themselves.

Another protection against picking up evil is wearing anklets of silver coins. Dimes are most popular and are given extra power if they are soaked for thirty minutes in the entrails of a living frog.

Other beliefs, though not as dramatic, were strictly adhered to. Indeed, the Gullah were subject to a code as strict as anything Leviticus or Deuteronomy imposed upon the Children of Israel. And like the Children wandering in the wilderness, the Gullah seized onto whatever they could for spiritual survival.

Some taboos, bad luck signs, and omens are as follows:

Never carry out ashes on Friday, or between Christmas and New Year's Day.

Never start a new task on Friday, or you will never finish it.

Never keep a crowing hen.

Never carry a hoe or spade into the house.

It is bad luck to lend matches, or pay back salt.

It is bad luck to dream of chickens.

A malfunctioning clock striking thirteen is a sure sign of impending death.

Never mend clothes while they are being worn.

It is bad luck to walk backwards, to sleep with hands

clasped behind the head.

Never shake left hands. It will put a curse on both persons.

If you start somewhere and have to go back because you forgot something, you must make an X in the road before you turn around.

A hooting owl is a bad omen. To quiet the owl, cross your fingers, take off a shoe and turn it over, point your finger in the direction of the sound, put a poker in the fire, and squeeze your right wrist with your left hand. If you are barefoot and outside, point your finger at the owl to cancel his power.

But there are good luck signs too. Some of them include the following:

Dreams of gray horses mean an upcoming happy marriage. Dreams of clear running water mean good luck and money.

If two people wash hands together, they will be friends forever. Burning onion peelings afterwards will strengthen the bond.

If you see a red bird on your doorstep, count to nine and money will follow.

Any bird singing on the doorstep means company is coming. The accidental dropping of a dishrag will hurry the arrival.

"Hoppin' John"—blackeyed peas, rice, and ham boiled together—eaten on New Year's Day will bring a prosperous year.

When you awaken on the first day of the month and say "rabbit" before you get out of bed, it will be a good month.

A piece of your lover's shirttail pinned to your skirt will keep him true.

A bit of cotton tied around an ankle will keep cramps away from a swimmer.

A bit of "magnetic sand" carried in a red flannel bag will bring money and good luck.

Wishes made to a new moon will come true, as will dreams beneath a new quilt.

Bubbles in coffee mean that money is on the way.

A nose full of snuff will quicken the labor of childbirth.

The first water taken by a new mother must be sipped from a thimble. This will ease the baby's first tooth.

Burn your old shoes and you will never suffer snakebite.

Burn your former lover's shoes and you will soon have more new ones than you have time for.

If you kill a snake in your yard, hang it from your porch post and your crops will never suffer drought.

A knot of "five finger" grass hung by the bed will make for restful sleep.

CHAPTER SIX

A Tale of Two Doctors

There are two giants in the history of South Carolina rootwork—two men: one black, one white—Dr. Buzzard, aka Stephaney Robinson, and The High Sheriff of the Lowcountry, aka J. E. McTeer.

Dr. Buzzard, master of a shadow world, lived his life in its shade. There are tales, legends, wild stories, but very few hard facts. His date of birth and the location of his grave remain mysteries. The reason for the first is simple: prior to 1915, the state of South Carolina made little attempt to keep birth records, especially of its African-American citizens. Birthdates were a private matter, usually journaled into family Bibles. The second—the location of the grave—is closely guarded by those few who may know. It is supposed, at the very least, the wholesale gathering of goofer dust from

the gravesite by countless believers would eventually result in a hole deep enough to uncover the remains. And then there are the remains themselves. A finger or toe bone from the famous Dr. Buzzard would be a priceless relic with enormous spiritual power. There is some supposition that the doctor was not buried at all but dismembered and passed around to other St. Helena Island root workers.

It is known, however, with reasonable certainty, that Dr. Buzzard died in early 1947 as a very old man. He received his mantle—his power—one legend asserts, from his father, who received it directly from a West African medicine man. Since importation of slaves was prohibited in the early 1800s, it would require an enormous generational stretch to assume Dr. Buzzard's father came from Africa. To be sure, the rising demand for slave labor resulted in widespread smuggling, most notably via Cuba, where importation was still legal. The last record of a smuggling attempt was the 1858 seizure of the slave sloop *Wanderer* off the coast of Charleston. On the other hand, diarist Laura Towne mentioned older slaves on St. Helena Island who still bore tribal marks and tattoos and still "worshiped with the moon, as their mothers had taught them."

Legend also says that when Dr. Buzzard's father—or grandfather, whatever the case may have actually been—arrived as a slave, his enormous power over other Africans soon became apparent to his owner, a local rice planter. The planter, afraid hexes and spells might have a negative

impact on his operation, granted this slave a piece of land and allowed him to live as a free man.

Writer Samuel Hopkins Adams encountered Dr. Buzzard on a Beaufort street in 1943, and described him thus: "At first sight, the elderly man might have been mistaken for a bishop in the A.M.E. (African Methodist-Episcopal) Church. He was tall, slightly bowed, benign of expression, and soberly dressed in quality black." Nothing too striking, to be sure. But what impressed Adams was the amount of quality merchandise the old man was loading into the car. Then there was the car itself: a shiny new Lincoln. And this was the second year of World War II, when new cars and consumer goods were nearly impossible to come by. Clearly, this Dr. Buzzard was a man of means.

And he was. Dr. Buzzard was known as a courtroom specialist, who could tip the scales of justice with spells, hexes, and roots; a predictor of winning numbers in clandestine lotteries; a dispenser of advice; and a controller of spirits. His clientele was nationwide and numbered in the tens of thousands.

Sam McGowan, who carried the mail on St. Helena Island for thirty-five years, remembered Dr. Buzzard's weekly trips to the St. Helena Island post office at Frogmore. Dr. Buzzard would open dozens upon dozens of letters in the lobby, quickly stuff the cash in his pockets. Money orders, which must be endorsed in order to cash, were torn up and deposited in a nearby trash can. Over the years, Dr. Buzzard

walked away from a fortune rather than incriminate himself with a signature.

His neighbors reported seeing license plates from seven states among the long line of cars parked in his driveway awaiting an audience.

Believing the story of Dr. Buzzard receiving his mantle from his forebears, the doctor himself claimed that he received his gift from a mockingbird. It lit on his head, he said, like the dove descending upon the head of Jesus, and, ever since, he had "the sight."

His fame as a conjurer was greatly enhanced after a party of Gullah fishermen drowned when a fierce and sudden squall overtook their small boat in St. Helena Sound. The fishing was good, the story goes, and the men had piled their catch into another boat. That second boat weathered the storm, and three days later, blew to shore with a buzzard aboard. The story spread that the buzzard had rowed the boat ashore. The Gullah took it as a sign.

Within a year or two the story—as stories often do—took on a life of its own. Dr. Buzzard, by this time, was doing business out of his home on Oaks Plantation, on the southwest corner of St. Helena Island. People as far away as Virginia swore that if a man wanted to see Dr. Buzzard, he could walk down to the creek bank and the doctor would send a boat propelled by two trained buzzards—one bird in the bow, another in the stern—and the buzzards would row with their wings. But watch out! If a man had trickery in

his heart—if he planned to deceive the doctor in any way—the buzzards would try to drown him!

In those days, the long arm of the law had an iron hand at its wrist. It was a reaction against the excesses of the post-Civil War Reconstruction era, when a cabal of Republican Yankees, Federal troops, and their allies among the freedmen pillaged the state treasury and made a mockery of the courts. The contested presidential election of 1876 between Tilden and Hayes went to the House of Representatives for a decision. The House, in turn, appointed an election commission to look into allegations of vote fraud, mostly in southern states, and to certify a winner.

Republican Hayes made southern Democrats a deal they could not refuse: in return for their support, he would pull out remaining garrisons of the hated Federal troops.

The deal was cut and delivered. Without the backing of Yankee bayonets, the carpetbagger rule collapsed. Former Confederate chief of cavalry Wade Hampton was elected governor, and rode to the governor's mansion with a pistol-packing entourage of his former troopers. Eleven years after Appomattox, the old Confederate leadership was again in power.

The election of Hampton coincided with the wholesale disenfranchisement of African-Americans throughout most of the South. The Gullah, however, were able to survive politically, mostly because many of them were "freeholders," owners of the land granted after the Yankee invasion of

1861. The right to vote, in those days, was determined by state, rather than Federal statute. In South Carolina, only property owners had that right. In 1878, it was estimated that there were some 1,500 African-American voters on St. Helena Island alone, more than in any other rural location in the United States.

Another factor in the survival of the Gullah community was the personality of Gov. Wade Hampton. Though he had once owned many slaves, he had often remarked that slavery was "a curse" upon the South, fostered by tradition and economic necessity. He had no hatred of African-Americans—so long as they voted for him! And many did, deserting the now impotent Republicans and joining the Democratic party in droves.

No matter how the Gullah voted, the white man eventually captured complete control of the district courts. Justice was swift and efficient, but also draconian. No one was "read his rights" upon arrest. The poor were not granted free legal counsel. *Habeas corpus* was just a funny term from a dead language. And "innocent until proven guilty" was a polite sarcasm. There were occasional and random sprinklings of justice, to be sure. If a person could afford it, he or she might have an even chance by hiring a slick white attorney—most Gullah farmers and fishermen could not.

The root doctor seemed a viable alternative to the expensive and incomprehensible workings of white legal counsel. A root concocted to be carried into court might cost

only ten dollars. For surer results, the root doctor might appear in person, liberally dosing the courtroom during recesses with goofer dust or various unknown powders. Particularly difficult cases might require casting the evil eye or chewing the root to intimidate witnesses and jury, if not His Honor himself.

Such a personal appearance by Dr. Buzzard or one of his colleagues would be expensive, often costing fully as much as an attorney's fee. But whereas an attorney's mysterious Latin phrases often did the accused no good at all, the root doctor's unknown tongues generally stopped the proceedings cold.

Immediately behind the Beaufort County Courthouse, stood the city water tower, an ancient and rusting spire, upon which a flock of buzzards had taken residence. Some days when sessions of court resulted in unusual human activity, the buzzards would take to the wing and soar high above the town, circling the tower and courthouse. It was a sure sign, the Gullah said, that Dr. Buzzard was at work.

Such was the milieu of Beaufort, South Carolina, in the 1920s. Into this seething cauldron of root, spell, and hex, stepped the new sheriff of Beaufort County, J. E. McTeer.

McTeer was from the oldest Carolina stock, a descendant of the Heywards, a family that had put pen to the Declaration of Independence. His maternal grandfather had been a slave-owning rice planter and had seen firsthand the

workings of African conjure men. His maternal grandmother was a poet and musician, but also a medium and
spiritualist. McTeer, as a young man, remembered a séance
in his grandparent's home where a heavy dining room table
wobbled, creaked, and groaned beneath his grandmother's
frail hands.

McTeer believed ESP, or second sight, is inherited,
much like left-handedness. He cited many examples of his
mother's gift and believed he inherited it also. Just as im-
portantly, he was raised in an environment where such spirituality was accepted as a precious gift. And it had a profound effect upon his thinking—and on his later life as well.

In 1926, McTeer's father, who had served as county
sheriff, died unexpectedly. County officials appointed young
Ed to fill the position.

As the new High Sheriff, Ed McTeer soon began running into troublesome cases. Healthy people took sick and
died for no apparent reason. Strange individuals showed up
in court, affixing potential witnesses with steely-eyed stares
that caused them to seize up in the middle of crucial testi-
mony. Mysterious white powder appeared on judges' and
prosecutors' desks. The High Sheriff suspected the work of
conjure men and decided he must learn more about the
phenomena if he was to effectively enforce the law in the
Gullah community. Dr. Buzzard, as the most famous conjure man, was targeted for surveillance. If a case could successfully be brought against the greatest, the sheriff hoped

lesser practitioners would be discouraged from further practice by example.

He recruited a local cab driver who regularly hauled out-of-town customers out to Dr. Buzzard's St. Helena Island home. But he had no sooner begun gathering intelligence, when the stream of information dried to a trickle, then to a few drops, finally to nothing at all. The cab driver explained, "They used to come back to the car ravin' 'bout how great Dr. Buzzard is. Now they ain't say nothin'."

Ed McTeer was convinced Dr. Buzzard's "second sight" had told him the law was on his trail. The sheriff tried other approaches, but to no avail.

World War II interrupted his plans to trap Dr. Buzzard. German submarines lay in wait just offshore, torpedoing shipping within sight of Charleston and Savannah. There were rumors of German spies slipping ashore in rubber boats. The Coast Guard recruited locals to ride horses up and down remote barrier island beaches and delegated Ed McTeer as their commander. Clearly, those concerns were more pressing than Dr. Buzzard's alleged unlicensed practice of medicine.

The High Sheriff was soon to change his mind.

The local draft board was sending busloads of young Gullah men to Fort Jackson just outside Columbia for induction into the Armed Forces. And Fort Jackson was sending nearly as many back as unfit, a majority with unexplained heart flutters and diarrhea. Ed McTeer suspected

Beaufort County's root doctors may have had something to do with it, and he stated so in a letter to the War Department. The War Department was predictably skeptical, filed the letter away, and promptly forgot all about it. But an event on October 26, 1943, changed their minds.

A busload of Gullah draftees set out for Fort Jackson from Hampton, South Carolina. One of them, a youth named Crispus Green, had assured his family of his prompt return. "Ain't goin' to no war," he said. "Dr. Buzzard, he fix me up."

He was not alone. Fully half the men on that bus had received tonics from various practitioners guaranteed to give them "hippity-hoppity hearts." They sang as the bus rolled on towards Fort Jackson:

> Gonna lay down my sword and shield,
> Down by the riverside, down by the riverside,
> Gonna lay down my sword and shield,
> Down by the riverside,
> Ain' gonna study war no mo'.

But before the bus reached Columbia, Crispus Green and another young man were dead. Half the others had to be rushed to the hospital. Now, the War Department was very interested—the FBI too.

McTeer was ordered to take leave of his coastal patrol and assist in the investigation. Though none of the afflicted

would dare to testify against a root doctor, Ed McTeer was able to obtain a small bottle of a mysterious potion. Analysis showed it contained moonshine whiskey and a small amount of lead arsenate. The local pharmacy's log showed a recent purchase of lead arsenate—not by Dr. Buzzard, as everyone had assumed, but by Dr. Bug, aka Peter Murray, of Laurel Bay Plantation.

Dr. Bug was arrested and brought before the court for an initial hearing, to enter a plea and to have bond set. It was a most interesting scene: a glowering Federal Magistrate, a triumphant Coast Guardsman and former sheriff, leering FBI men, and Dr. Bug, whom Adams described as a "timorous, dull-eyed, and shambling old man."

Dr. Bug made no effort to defend himself. Of course he had dispensed the potion. "Them boys shouldn't have to fight no war if they don' want," he said. "No, that potion ain't pizen. I drinks a shot of it myself ever'day. I'll drink some right now to prove it," he said, pointing at Exhibit A on the magistrate's bench.

The court, fearing the loss of crucial evidence—or of the defendant himself—refused the offer. A guilty plea was accepted. Next came the matter of a bond. Could the prisoner pay one?

"Why, yes," Dr. Bug said. "Bring me my box."

Bailiffs wrestled a good sized trunk into the courtroom. Dr. Bug opened it and asked how much he owed. The magistrate set bail at a thousand dollars. Dr. Bug began passing

bills to the bailiff—twenties, tens, and an unending stream of soiled and wrinkled dollar bills, until the debt was satisfied.

Dr. Bug made ready to take his leave but was interrupted by an official of the Internal Revenue Service, of which the doctor had never heard. The official confiscated two thousand dollars for taxes.

Dr. Bug limped back to Laurel Bay and took to his bed. He abandoned his practice and pined away, convinced someone in Washington, D.C., had put the root on him. Legend says he died soon afterwards.

But Dr. Buzzard remained a free man. He was brought in for questioning on the draft avoidance matter, but no one would testify against him. So the case had to be dismissed without trial. After the war, Ed McTeer took up the trail once again.

The break came after a suspect in a burglary case had been discovered in possession of a root and a mysterious white powder. Ed McTeer suspected that both had originated with Dr. Buzzard. When McTeer donned blue sunglasses, the suspect broke down and confessed all. The root, he related, was supposed to make him invisible and the powder was to be taken to prevent his arrest. He had received both from Dr. Buzzard. The sheriff held the suspect in custody and sent word for Dr. Buzzard to come in for questioning.

The doctor arrived in due time, affecting an imperious

air worthy of his status. Ed McTeer ushered the suspect into the room and began the interrogation. He had not proceeded very far, however, before Dr. Buzzard donned his blue glasses and affixed the eyes of the accused. The suspect began to shake, to groan, to beat himself all over like he was covered with stinging ants. He fell to the floor, thrashing and rolling, his eyes rolling back into his head, and frothing at the mouth. McTeer could plainly see that the suspect would never be able to testify against Dr. Buzzard, so he had his deputies take him back to his cell.

"Are you through with me?" the doctor asked.

The sheriff acknowledged that he was beaten temporarily, but eventually he would find a witness Dr. Buzzard could not hex.

"You do your job and I'll do mine," the doctor said as he left.

Shortly thereafter, McTeer encountered Dr. Buzzard in court, where he sat among the spectators, murmuring and casting his eyes malevolently on the judge, jury, and prosecutor, trying to hex the proceedings so several accused persons would be found innocent. After the noon recess, he returned to the courtroom to find an unknown white powder sprinkled generously around the judge's chair. He went outside and found Dr. Buzzard resting in the shade.

"Dr. Buzzard," he said, "I know you are trying to root this court. If you persist, I will have you bound over for contempt."

"I hear you," the doctor said, noncommittally.

A few weeks later, McTeer received word via an informant that Dr. Buzzard had been highly offended by that threat and that full-scale spiritual warfare had commenced.

"You remind him," the sheriff told the informant, "that I have the power too, and trouble is very close to him."

In an effort to remove a symbol of Dr. Buzzard's influence on the court, McTeer took a rifle to the buzzards roosting on the city water tower. His first shot flew true. Climbing the tower several days later to remove the carcass, he found a recent storm had blown away the tower's wooden roof, and the dead bird had fallen into the city's water supply. Another victory for the doctor!

But Ed McTeer's luck was soon to change. Shortly after the water tower incident, Dr. Buzzard's son—who regularly smashed the expensive cars his daddy bought him—was heading home in a blinding rainstorm, when he ran off one of the many causeways that cross the Beaufort County's tidal marshes and was drowned in a saltwater creek. Believing his son's death was a direct result of Ed McTeer's hex, Dr. Buzzard called a truce.

The sheriff returned home one afternoon to find Dr. Buzzard awaiting him—in the best West African tradition—with a peace offering of two live chickens. "You and I are too powerful to fight any longer," the doctor said.

McTeer offered his sympathies for the death of Dr. Buzzard's son, but stopped short of either denying respon-

sibility or apologizing. He did, however, offer to stop practicing black magic, if the doctor would stop prescribing potions. Dr. Buzzard accepted the terms. "I'll stop the medicine but I will keep working spells. I'll put them on and you take them off—if you can."

And so the deal was cut.

But it did not last. Soon enough, Dr. Buzzard was back in court—this time as a defendant indicted for the old occupational hazard of root doctoring: practicing medicine without a license.

Dr. Buzzard was in a dilemma. Should he, as his friends and family urged, hire another practitioner to chew the root on his behalf, as he had done for countless others? Or should he go out and hire a slick white lawyer? He chose the latter option, retaining a respected state senator who maintained a private practice.

Ultimately, conventional legal help did him no good. Though his lawyer argued the charges were trumped up because of the government's grudge over its prior failure to get an indictment for aiding draft avoidance, the court found the doctor guilty and fined him three hundred dollars. Dr. Buzzard paid it on the spot, peeling the bills out of his well-stuffed pockets.

But the conviction took the steam out of Dr. Buzzard. Soon he was bedridden. A medical doctor was called and pronounced the diagnosis: cancer of the stomach. He died soon afterwards.

The High Sheriff of the Lowcountry, J. E. McTeer—white root doctor for fifty years and archenemy of the famous Dr. Buzzard—stands by his voodoo altar. Courtesy of Thomas McTeer.

The message to the Gullah was as plain as day. Two men messed with the government and both of them were dead. Obviously, there was a powerful root doctor working way up there in Washington, D.C.

Ed McTeer remained in law enforcement and rootwork for another twenty years. In the 1960s, he was challenged in the polls by a South Carolina Highway Patrol sergeant.

The campaign was a long and bitter one, with innuendo, rumor, and allegations flying from both sides: The highway patrolman had attempted to sexually molest a woman while her husband was away deer hunting; Ed McTeer's deputies habitually took bribes from Gullah bootleggers; the sheriff regularly took the county chain gang out to work his Coffin Point plantation. The charges and countercharges finally attracted so much attention that a Charleston television station agreed to a debate, of sorts.

Though they were afraid to have the armed antogonists face each other before the cameras, each would read a half-hour-long campaign speech over the air. Ed McTeer cited his forty years of public service, his extensive experience, his respect for the community, black and white alike. But the following evening, when the challenger's response was to be aired, television screens all over the Lowcountry dissolved into a flutter, buzz, and blur of interference, the *root* apparently affecting modern communication as well as all other forms of human endeavor.

Such mysterious impediments notwithstanding, the

challenger managed to unseat Ed McTeer by a thin margin. McTeer retired from public life to write his memoirs, including the outstanding *Fifty Years as a Lowcountry Witch Doctor*. Though courted by the national media, he steadfastly refused to talk further about his rootwork in public.

The victorious highway patrolman went on to a stormy tenure as sheriff, the highlight of which occurred his last week in office, when he assaulted a grand jury foreman—a retired brigadier general, no less—then barricaded himself in his home, threatened suicide, then ripped the telephone from the wall. Both coroner and undertaker were notified, but the new sheriff was extracted without incident and re-

McTeer at work on his memoirs, *The High Sheriff of the Lowcountry* and *Fifty Years as a Lowcountry Witch Doctor*.
Courtesy of Thomas McTeer.

ferred to a psychologist, which incidently, did him little good. Knowledgeable locals expected it all along. The High Sheriff was a proud man and had not taken kindly to defeat. A slow-working root had driven the new sheriff into insanity.

Ed McTeer died in 1976. A daughter handles the sale of his books, which continue to fascinate. His youngest son has begun to dabble in his father's work and is one of the few—if not the only—white rootworkers in Beaufort County. Apparently, his work fills an important social niche. Recently, he had to concoct two lucky roots and rush them to the airport in Savannah, forty miles away. Two clients steadfastly refused to board their plane without them!

Dr. Buzzard's mantle passed to his son-in-law, who plied his trade at Oaks Plantation on St. Helena Island, the site of the old master's original conjurations, until his death in 1997. Friends, neighbors, and clients honored him with the nickname "Buzzy."

Though it is unsure exactly who has taken over Buzzy's practice, someone most likely has.

Why It Works

The root, some say, works simply because people believe it works. Science writer David Cohen succinctly stated such in his summary of paranormal doings, *Voodoo, Devils, and a New Invisible World*: "In a society that believes in witchcraft, witchcraft works."

That belief in South Carolina, and across the entire South as well, appears to be widespread and is categorized according to degree. Much like varying degrees of Christian devoutness, there is active belief, when a person daily considers its spiritual tenants and conducts himself or herself accordingly; passive belief, wherein a person considers its truth a distinct possibility; and crisis belief, when a person seeks refuge there after all else appears to have failed.

Estimates of active belief among the Gullah at the turn

of the century ran as high as ninety percent; of crisis belief, at close to one hundred. The Gullah are also almost universally devout Christians and that Christianity serves as a vehicle for, rather than an impediment to, rootwork. After all, witches and conjurers are mentioned in the Bible. As one Gullah preacher said, "Any man who don't believe in witches don't believe in God."

Belief among Carolina whites, while not as prevalent as among the Gullah, is certainly widespread, perhaps as high as half of the population. Though not many whites seek out a root doctor's services, and there are very few white rootworkers, no white man or woman would consciously put himself or herself on the wrong side of a hex. And if hexed, many would seek appropriate expertise to have the spell removed.

Belief among both races waned mid-century. A treasury of spiritual folklore gathered in the 1960s by a group of students at Beaufort's all-black Robert Smalls Senior High School was carefully prefaced with a disclaimer: This may have been believed by their parents and grandparents, but these students took no stock in such notions.

But things change, coming full circle as they often do. There appears to be a belief growing once again as many impatient people look for an expansion of spirituality beyond the confines of mainline conservative Christianity. Perhaps a growing unease with the coming of the new millennium has contributed to an increased interest in the

possibilities of rootwork. Whatever the reason, root doctors continue to attract a loyal clientele, and that clientele appears to be growing. Crisis belief among the Gullah may be almost universal once again. And among South Carolina whites, it easily surpasses fifty percent.

This is hardly surprising, considering the many documented and well-known histories of the power of the conjure. One outstanding example occurred on St. Helena Island in the late 1950s. A man experienced a general decline in health and fortune, accompanied by shooting pains in his legs—a sure sign, he believed, that an enemy had buried an evil root on his property and he had been infected by walking over it daily. He began a campaign to locate and remove the root, working on his own rather than retaining a competing doctor.

He began by digging up the earth around his steps and, finding nothing, expanded his efforts to the front yard. Daily he dug, as his health deteriorated. Though his steadily declining health began to limit his activities, he dug and dug, eventually spading up his entire holding, more than an acre. Finally, he could dig no more and took to his bed, where death eventually overtook him.

After the funeral, his daughter—still convinced the root remained undiscovered—set fire to the house! The resulting pall of back smoke, rising above St. Helena's pines and palmettos and sliding down the sea wind, alerted the neighbors for miles around—and made a powerful impression that was

to last for generations. Insurance, if there was any, would not pay off on a house deliberately burned. And here was a woman willing to sacrifice all of what little she had to foil the power of a deadly hex.

Nowhere in human experience does the mind play such a role as in sexuality. If the brain does not work, nothing else will—in a man, especially. Vengeful Gullah women have often used conjuring to foil their mates' wandering inclinations. Such an incident occurred in Beaufort in the early 1960s. A man announced his intentions to leave his wife and marry another. She obtained a mysterious white powder from a root doctor and during a spirited discussion with her departing husband, took a pair of his shorts from the laundry and dusted them thoroughly. "You may leave me," she said, "an' I can't stop you from goin', but you'll never be a man to that woman!" With that she laughed and threw his shorts into the stove. The man left and pursued his intentions, eventually obtaining a divorce and remarrying. But after nearly a year into his new relationship, he was still unable to perform sexually. His new wife left him and he committed suicide by shooting himself in the head with a revolver.

Chalk up another victim to a rootwork hex.

Ed McTeer, in spite of his belief in his own extrasensory abilities, thought the power of the root was entirely linked to what he termed "auto-suggestion." A person, he said, must believe or the root would have no power.

Perhaps.

But that belief need not be active. If a person should intellectualize that there just might be something to it, much like he or she might speculate about the possibility of intelligent life somewhere in the vastness of space, that would be enough to start the root working. Then, if the slightest misfortune, like any one of the myriad petty annoyances that daily plague all of humankind, should only slightly reinforce the notion of evil afoot, the next misfortune would be noted with increased consternation. And thus, not-so-fearsome events become fearsome and pile upon others, until the individual becomes overwhelmed by mounting catastrophes with an ultimate negative effect on health.

Ed McTeer, imbued with a paternalism spawned in the plantation era, tended to look upon the Gullah as "his people." His self-assumed responsibilities went beyond the enforcement of the letter of the law—as evident in his battles with Dr. Buzzard over the integrity of District Court—to a consideration for the Gullah's general welfare. If someone had been rooted and was suffering, he took it upon himself to undo the hex before the afflicted died.

Thus came about "the McTeer method," which he fine-tuned and successfully practiced for nearly fifty years. In 1962, before his political defeat soured him on public appearances, he related an example of such activities in a speech before a Beaufort civic group.

There was an old Gullah woman under the influence

of an evil root who, in Gullah terminology, had "wizened and waned" until she was near death. McTeer showed up, unannounced, at her doorstep one Saturday to perform an exorcism. The old woman was too weak to get out of bed and McTeer needed room for his showmanship, so he summoned family and neighbors and had them haul the woman, cot and all, out onto the front porch. McTeer put on his blue sunglasses—the conjure man's badge of office—and began his spiel.

He knew, he said, speaking from his position in the front yard, that there was evil working on this place—he could feel it in his bones. God had given him the gift of clairvoyance and prophecy. Though he was powerful enough to use the gift for evil, he had sworn only to use it for good, and he was going to use it, right then, to cure the afflicted woman.

The object of the cure was nonplussed. She lay, immobile and impassive, entirely resigned to impending death—though McTeer noted she was watching him from the corner of one eye. McTeer then went into a "trance," circling the yard, his arms and legs trembling, his head thrown back. Unbeknownst to the woman and the rapt audience on the porch, McTeer had previously visited the site under cover of darkness and had planted a blue root beneath the front steps. He circled and circled, muttering incomprehensible unknown tongues, noticing that he now had the woman's undivided attention. She had risen to one elbow and was

watching the proceedings with considerable interest.

Finally, McTeer howled and dove for the steps, coming up with the root. He waved it aloft in a show of victory. At the sight of the dreaded object, the spectators recoiled in horror, then shouted hallelujahs and hosannas of praise, as McTeer stumbled to the edge of the yard and flung the offending root far out into the flowing waters of a tidal creek—for that was one way to cancel a blue root's power; the other being to throw it into a fiery stove, but, in this case, that would have necessitated bringing it into the house and further terrifying the victim.

McTeer returned to the house the following week to find the woman up and around, eating, cleaning, cooking as usual. She had been saved from sure death; the county was spared the trouble of a pointless and inconclusive investigation, the family of needless funeral expenses, the malevolent root doctor of another success.

Incidentally, both the woman and her entire family would cast their votes for the High Sheriff until he chose to retire.

McTeer repeated such performances many times, no doubt saving dozens who otherwise would have surely died.

Such showmanship and auto-suggestion are dubious contributions to the hexing and curing of a prominent—and white—Beaufort attorney a number of years ago. The man had hired a Gullah housekeeper, but then dismissed her because he found her surly and unmotivated. The woman

had left the house in a huff, muttering about mouthing or rooting her former employer. A new woman was hired, and her first day on the job discovered three new sewing needles tied in a bundle with black thread stuck between the couple's mattress. The maid recognized it as a suffering root, threw the needles into the stove, and urged the attorney's wife to seek immediate help from a root doctor.

The wife laughed the incident off—until the following morning when she awoke to find her skin covered with a scaly rash. She then sought help, not from a conjure man but from a medical specialist in Charleston. The diagnosis: a severe bout of chicken pox, the worst the doctor had ever seen. A day later, her infant son also came down with the pox. A month later, they had both recovered, but her husband was stricken with severe abdominal pain. He was rushed to the hospital for an emergency appendectomy. An older son was already there for a long-scheduled removal of his tonsils. During the operation, something went wrong. The boy stopped breathing and was revived only after much effort by panicked nurses. Both father and son eventually went home, but their troubles were far from over.

The attorney suffered a long series of debilitating post-operative infections. On one visit to his physician, he was struck by the similarity between the stitches still retaining his infected incision and the black thread bundling the needles found beneath his mattress. He demanded their immediate removal. The physician protested. It was too early, especially

considering infection had delayed the healing process. The attorney insisted and the doctor complied. Two days later, the attorney was completely healed. Neither he nor any member of his family suffered any further inexplicable and catastrophic ailments.

The attorney, trained in the rational process and having worked for years in the logical legal argument, had trouble making sense of what happened to him and his family. He had never been a believer in any sort of paranormal activities and was especially contemptuous of "Negro folktales." Yet his personal experience cried out for explanation—one he was never able to give. Reflecting on the incident, the most he would say was, "I may not believe in roots now, but I will no longer scoff at them." Such a grudging acceptance of the possibilities of evil rootwork puts him in a class with most of his peers. He has a tiny seed of belief in his heart and is thus forever subject to the power of the root.

Folklorists and ethnologists, in various attempts to explain the workings of the root, have taken a cue from mythologist J.G. Frazer, author of the famed *Golden Bough*. Frazer categorized conjuring, magic, and myth into two types that very conveniently fit into slots in the human mental machinery and allow the mind and the spirit ascendancy over flesh and logic.

There is the "law of similarity," in which like produces like. An example of this would be the tale about the famed

Dr. Buzzard receiving his power when a mockingbird lit upon his head. The mockingbird is an aggressive nester, driving all others from his domain. He is also a raucous mimic, assuming the persona of other birds, even of automobiles, telephones, and trains, speaking in "other tongues." The human-animal parallel is obvious. Also working here is the powerful Christian symbol, the baptism of Jesus in the River Jordan by John. The spirit of God, the scripture says, descended upon the head of Jesus like a dove, itself an example of the law of similarity.

Frazer's second concept is the "law of contact." Here, objects that were once connected remain so, even if removed. Thus, part of a person can be used to affect him or her at a distance. A "follow me root" will have additional power if it is sewed up in a piece of the lover's clothes. Various death roots will be particularly effective if they contain a bit of hair or a snip of fingernail from the intended victim.

Evil roots combining both concepts can be particularly heinous. For instance, the combination of a fingernail with a bone from a black dog might make the afflicted fall to his hands and knees, defecate upon the floor, and howl at the full moon. The addition of lizard bones will cause hallucinations of that animal crawling upon the flesh. There are even reports of boils and sores erupting with little snakes and salamanders.

Though the skeptic may wish to dismiss the wildest of

such tales, it has been widely documented that people indeed die from roots, hexes, and the riding of the merciless hags.

Behavioral science has done a poor job explaining the ability of a root to heal or kill. While scientific journals occasionally mention hex-related death, there seems to be an inability—or an unwillingness—to plunge into the necessary fieldwork to document hormonal changes resulting from a successful deathwish. Ironically, science has not gone much further than drowning rats and attempting to draw human parallels. This phenomenon, in rats at least, is known as "the sudden death syndrome."

The experiment went something like this: A number of rats were immersed in cold water. Some drowned right away, others swam for two or more hours before drowning. All rats were thoroughly examined after death. The rats that swam for a prolonged period before succumbing, died of exhaustion and inhalation of water, as might be expected. The rats that died immediately were found to have succumbed to stress-induced heart failure.

After that discovery, a second batch of rats were drowned. But this second batch was exposed to drowning conditions on several occasions before their final plunge. A much higher percent of these rats died from stress-induced heart failure. The conclusion: the second flotilla of rats believed they were doomed and subsequently willed themselves to die.

Examples of the event in humans cite "a profound arousal" of the sympathetic nervous system leading to a disastrous fall in blood pressure. "In these cases," one report proclaims, "they might well die in a true state of shock—in the surgical sense—a shock induced by prolonged and intense emotion" resulting in rapid and erratic heart rate that can lead to heart failure and death.

These reports ignore the almost total absence of such stress-related deaths in other, extremely stressful but non-conjured, situations. Though persons with chronic heart conditions are apt to die suddenly during earthquakes, tornadoes, or hurricanes, healthy hostages remain in captivity for months under daily threat of death and do not die. Thousands of individuals, indeed entire urban populations, have been confined in air raid shelters and bombed daily for months, without wholesale stress-induced deaths. Fanatical Japanese troops holed up in caves during World War II were widely assumed to have been "scared to death" after they were faced with American flame throwers. Subsequent investigation, however, indicated they had died when flames had sucked the oxygen from their hiding places. Human beings, it seems, living under the most brutalizing and terrifying conditions, prove amazingly resilient—if no hexes are involved.

Science, in this case at least, seems to be at an even greater handicap than Justice. Justice may be blind, but Science seems almost autistic by comparison.

CHAPTER
EIGHT

A Village of Believers

In 1970, dancer and artist Walter S. King left his native Detroit with a nightmare and a dream. The nightmare was his perceived failure of the Civil Rights movement. All the gains touted by proponents of integration and equal opportunity were illusions, he believed, resulting in only a few token concessions by the majority culture and a slight improvement in the economic conditions of African-Americans. The dream was to rediscover his African roots. He headed south in a battered pickup truck, with $38 in cash and a stack of used masonite sheeting.

Walter King did not find his roots among the Gullah of the Carolina coast. Bypassing the remnants of the slave culture entirely, he reached back to Nigeria, from which his ancestors had come. Those roots lay deep in the history of

the long-gone Yoruba Empire and its religion known as Ifa.

Ifa leads its devotees to higher consciousness, to a one-ness with all Creation, by teaching a system of ethics, religious belief, and mystic vision. This spiritual journey, called *irin ajo*, seeks to unite earthly consciousness, *Ori*, with heavenly consciousness, the *Iponri*. A devotee enlists the aid of ancestral spirits to help along the way and, in so doing, finds spiritual destiny, his or her *ayanmo*.

These tenets were first set down some 4,000 years ago by Orunmila, the Moses of the Ifa faith. The Yoruba insist that Orunmila did not originate these teachings, for these were truths in existence before the beginning of the world. Orunmila collected them, encoded them, and passed them on to his spiritual descendants. In fact, the Yoruba believe their religion to be the original religion of humans on earth.

Yoruba folklore says Orunmila was a sickly child from a remote village—"a little boy with a big head"—possibly handicapped with some congenital defect. But Orunmila more than made up in spirit what he lacked in the flesh. His parents and neighbors recognized early his proclivity in spiritual matters and gave him a name that, literally translated, means "Only Heaven Knows the Way to Salvation."

Legend says Orunmila was tutored by sixteen angelic elders who were sent to earth by God Himself. With their help, Orunmila—like Buddha—was able to achieve divine status. And, like Jesus, he exists today at the right hand of God.

Ifa spread throughout Africa—first by conquest, later by the enslavement of its devotees. Religious historians note Ifa's influence on other world religions. Indeed, its thirteen commandments—including honor and respect of elders, prohibitions against breaking covenants, stealing, and adultery—are quite similar to the ten brought down from Mt. Sinai by Moses. There is even speculation that Yorubas were enslaved by the Egyptians during the same years the Children of Israel suffered in bondage, and that cross-cultural exchanges were likely.

Walter King eventually settled on ten South Carolina acres near the village of Sheldon, some fourteen miles north of Beaufort, where he became King Adefumi I of the Village of Oyotunji. He tried to forget the nightmare, to live the dream. There would be communal living, farming of traditional crops by traditional means, shrines and temples, a school where children would learn Yoruba language and custom and Ifa religious practices—including ritual animal sacrifice, divination, and polygamy. Though men and women were to live separately, the king declared a man might have as many wives as he could support. He himself, was eventually to have eight. But the union need not be sexual. Wives could be held for political and social reasons, or if they had no other man to protect or support them.

King Adefumi was soon joined by others, teachers, artisans, students, jobless college graduates, troublesome urban children sent to his care by despairing parents. The popu-

lation of Oyotunji Village soon reached 170. It wasn't long before King Adefumi declared the village an independent nation, and posted a sign at the village gate: "You are now leaving the United States."

Predictably, Adefumi has strained the tolerance of his neighbors. The Gullah were incredulous, believing the village was demonstrating an undoing of all they had gained in their long struggle up from slavery. Whites were openly hostile. Reports of the goings-on in King Adefumi's domain were whispered around the community and reported to various authorities.

The authorities refused to become involved. None of the king's eight marriages were recorded at the county courthouse, so the sheriff elected not to bring bigamy charges. The Department of Public Health decided not to measure the distance between the village pump and a row of privies unless there were documentable health problems. A physician with the community health program—himself a native of Nigeria—found the villagers' health to be on par with other locals. The private school, which educates village children in the ancient African tradition, was exempt from official scrutiny because the Legislature had long ago sought to facilitate the formation of private all-white schools by removing mandates and state overview of curriculum. And what was good enough for white parents seeking an all-white education for their children was certainly valid for African-Americans. Even radical animal rights advocates

were afraid to contest sacrificial rites since it might be deemed an interference with villagers' religious freedom. For similar reasons, the scarring of young children with three "tribal marks" on each cheek has failed to bring any charge of child abuse.

So, the most neighbors could do was grumble about the few villagers receiving food stamps (reparations for slavery, the king says,) and gossip and giggle about polygamy. And they soon tired of that and resigned themselves to "the voodoo village," as they had chosen to call it.

Mary C. Martin, a home economist from Charlotte, North Carolina, is not so passive. After "rescuing" her son from the influence of Adefumi, she stated vehement opposition. "It's an eyesore, a canker to human development and family living, a disservice to the people of Beaufort, South Carolina, and the nation."

Henry James, a native of Philadelphia, came seeking the Nigerian connection. He had visited there and always longed to go back. But he didn't find what he was seeking at Oyotunji. "I looked around at the plastic chairs, the cars, the electricity. Maybe this is one man's dream to have the world the way he wants it, but it just doesn't seem real to me."

The village supports itself—as much as it is able—through tourism and by performing a number of Ifa rites for hire. Because it considers itself a sovereign state, there is even a "Minister of Tourism," Her Grace Iya Shanla

Odufonda, King Adefumi's "First Wife."

"We are trying to recreate the Yoruba lifestyle," the king said in a recent interview, "to build houses, to earn a living. This prevents us from producing any real competence in farming. People prefer to be philosophers rather than farmers." To this end, the village publishes a home page on the World Wide Web. The Web page offers bits of news from the village, wisdom from the ancient Yorubas, and "readings" divined by village priests while entranced. Typical of such readings are the following, offered for African-Americans, all Americans, or the entire world by the king, himself, Babalawo Adefumi I, Baale of Oyotunji, South Carolina:

> "Owonrin' Yeku—African Americans will be surrounded by ancient and immediate ancestral spirits of all types who will mass themselves about, listening to all types of ideas, thoughts, and inspirations. Their presence will be uncanny and myriad, showing themselves in great numbers."

Or, menacingly:

> "Ogunda' Fun (Kotojale)—Osobo can only be relieved by planning for a larger military venture than anticipated along with plenty of

dogged hard work. Lots of frustrated efforts but must carry on with persistence . . . be cautious of trouble, confusion, disarray, anger, and people who are totally undisciplined."

Typical of the rituals performed at the village is the following recorded in a local newspaper. It was "the feeding of the head," the culmination of the training of four women from Las Vegas and Miami inducted into the Ifa faith as priestesses:

> "The ritual was performed in a six-columned peristyle next to the king's residence. Each woman wore a long white robe, and cowry shells, a symbol of prosperity, were woven into their braided hair.
>
> "The four women stood silently, smoking large cigars as the king's assistant brushed various points of their bodies with the intended sacrifice—live chickens.
>
> "The king's assistant handed each one a chicken and showed them how to pluck a few feathers from each side. He then waved the squawking and flapping chickens around their heads.
>
> "Next the king took the sacrifice from a priestess, turned to a series of white porcelain

vessels and with a quick stroke, cut off its head. The stream of blood flowing from its neck was poured into the vessels.

"Still holding the chicken by its feet, Adefumi turned and placed blood on the woman's feet, hands, arms, shoulders, and tongue. The women knelt over the vessels, still smoking their cigars, while the king tossed coconut shells to devine their future."

King Adefumi offers another service: help for those hauled before District Court. Unlike Dr. Buzzard, the famed courtroom specialist, King Adefumi does not appear in court in person. But, for a fee, he will perform a ceremony to give strength, wisdom, and eloquence to an accused person's attorney. And there are also rituals, in the finest tradition of root doctoring, that have shown success in retrieving lost love.

Village population has declined in recent years, down to only thirty-five permanent residents. Many who come are from the city and soon become disenchanted with primitive living—the weeding, chopping, hauling of water—that is a grinding daily routine of rural life in developing countries. But nearly thirty years into his venture, King Adefumi remains true to his dream. There will come a time, he believes, when there will be a wholesale migration of African-Americans from urban centers. They will come seeking their

roots in an Afro-centric rural lifestyle. And the village will be ready—ready to teach them survival skills and ancestral ways. The king has even designated his successor, should he not live to see it. It is his son, His Royal Lordship Prince Adeg Balu.

Searching for Dr. Buzzard

*"Can you imagine being a conjureman in possession
of a boxful of Dr. Buzzard's metacarpals?
You could be elected mayor of Savannah!"*

It was early Spring of 1997. I was in the city of my
birth—Beaufort, South Carolina—on a mission bordering on
obsession. I was looking for the grave of the famous Dr.
Buzzard.

Dr. Buzzard, aka Stephaney Robinson, was a
conjureman, a root doctor, a courtroom specialist who
could tip the scales of justice with spells and hexes; a predictor of winning numbers in clandestine lotteries; a dispenser of advice; a controller of spirits; a man who literally
held the power of life and death in the nod of his head, the
blink of his eye. His clientele was fearful, adoring, and na-

131

tionwide, numbering in the tens of thousands.

Dr. Buzzard died when I was yet in the cradle, but I heard the legends and wild stories as a boy: Dr. Buzzard receiving his power when a mockingbird descended on his head like the dove upon Jesus; Dr. Buzzard tearing up a fortune in postal money orders rather than incriminate himself with endorsements; Dr. Buzzard keeping hundreds of young black men out of World War II by giving them "hippity-hoppity hearts"; Dr. Buzzard first hexing the local sheriff into inactivity, then later becoming his mentor when he knew his own time was short.

That conflict turned collaboration was the subject of a magazine article I published in the fall of 1995. Then the phone started ringing. Radio talk show hosts from Denver, San Diego, Montreal, even Johannesburg—all wanted to talk about Dr. Buzzard and his deadliest hex, the dreaded blue root. The blue root, prepared with graveyard dirt gathered at midnight, was known to cause wells and cows to go dry, chickens to cease laying, misfortune to mount misfortune, to precipitate miserable disability, and finally bring most welcome death.

Soon enough, I was at work on a book. Since such a book would severely stretch the limits of credulity, it cried out for pictures that would not lie. A photo of Dr. Buzzard's grave was surely in order. Verily, would an author of a work on Thomas Jefferson, Robert E. Lee, even Al Capone, offer his readers less?

Beaufort is a languorous island town of 15,000, exuding a gentility reminiscent of the antebellum South. Breezy, white-columned verandas overlook the sweeping bend of a lazy tidal river, spreading oaks and magnolias filter sunlight that falls into lush and pungent gardens of camellia, honeysuckle, and jasmine. Clock time plays second fiddle to sun time and tide time. Residents sip iced tea in the shade, and the conversation seldom gets beyond a strenuous argument over who is going to get up and bring more.

St. Helena Island is two bridges and twelve miles away. It's another world—a Gullah world. The Gullah, grandsons and granddaughters of slaves, unwilling builders of an empire, were given land and freedom by the conquering Yankee Army. They have endured and sometimes nearly prospered. Their musical patois, toothsome cuisine, and unlikely amalgamation of African and Christian religion powerfully spice a unique island reality. . . . That's where I would look for Dr. Buzzard.

I began with my own father, former coroner of Beaufort County. My father had seen it all, a grisly forty-year parade of car wrecks, drownings, murder, and mayhem. Though he occasionally encountered deaths by hex, ("dead of undetermined natural causes," he would write on those certificates), Dr. Buzzard had died of stomach cancer—no violence or mystery there—thus the coroner was not involved. There, I hit my first of many dead ends.

But like all the other "dead ends," a little bit of life

remained—just enough to send me careening off in another direction.

My father mentioned an old classmate of mine, formerly the most notorious poacher and fish hog among my circle of dubious acquaintances, who had lately repented of his ways and become a game warden. The warden had been digging into this Dr. Buzzard business himself and had come around asking my father the same question. Maybe the warden could help.

Wardens in those parts, occasionally being subject to the extreme displeasure of their clientele, do not list their home telephone numbers. I asked around and found he was keeping company with a certain woman. Her number was in the book. A machine answered. I left a message.

I left another, and yet another. Two days later, I gave up on voice mail and considered my alternatives. I would fish without a license, I decided, drop a deer in plain view of a major highway. Surely that would warrant his attention.

Instead, I called another friend who had also gone to school with Warden Incommunicado.

Oh yes, he said, he knew where Dr. Buzzard was buried. No, he hadn't actually seen the grave, but he heard it was over in the woods across from the water tower, out on US 21.

I knew the spot, five hundred tangled acres of prime rattlesnake habitat. Armed with camera and a long forked stick, I embarked on safari. Six hours later, I had sore feet

and a veritable infestation of chiggers. But no snake bites. And no Dr. Buzzard.

I bemoaned my failure over spirits—liquid spirits. Another friend said, "I bet he's buried in a churchyard." I was skeptical. Would they bury a conjureman—*a witchdoctor*—in holy ground? My friend laughed, "Would they dare not to?"

I asked around. A blind man at the Seaside Grocery knew everything, said nothing. He looked right through me with his milky eyeballs, flashed a metallic grin, shook his head. "Boy, why you wan' mess 'round wif dat stuff?" An old crone hobbled from a shanty, slapped her thigh, cackled at my request. The white people I had asked didn't know. These people knew but wouldn't say. I was getting closer.

Another evening, another round of spirits, another friend. "How long you been looking for this Buzzard feller?"

"Three days."

"Why don't you just give up?"

In my checkered career as a journalist, I had interviewed tax evaders, dope smugglers, gun runners, felons all. They *all* talked. Damned if I would be stonewalled by a conjureman—a dead one, at that!

Another trip back into rattlesnake heaven. Same results. Driving around, scratching chigger bites, I chanced upon a mobile home raised above regular storm tides on tall cement block posts. I climbed onto the porch and knocked. "Any old burying grounds in this neighborhood?"

The man looked off into middle distance. Not that he recalled. "Who you all looking for?"

I drew a breath, took a chance. "Dr. Buzzard."

The man's eyes rolled like tumblers in an old time slot machine, but his response was immediate. "Why, he ain't dead!"

Great God Almighty! I nearly fell off the porch. Reeling, I asked for an explanation. No, it wasn't another Resurrection. The mantle had been passed to a family member. My informant was about my age, too young to have known the original doctor, assumed this new one was the only one, pushing the ripe old age of 150 years. I asked directions and, surprisingly enough, got them—along with the new doctor's legal name.

But the new doctor was not in. Others were waiting. A car with Georgia plates sat idling in the shade. One from Virginia passed me on the way out.

I called later that evening, got the new doctor on the phone. I identified myself, asked my perennial question.

"You gonna dig him up?" he questioned.

Why no, I had no intentions of exhumation.

"Then why you want to know?"

I explained, but the new doctor was unimpressed by my motives or credentials. "He buried out in the bush" was the most I could get out of him.

I made another call—to an artist who had made his name and fortune capturing the essence of the Carolina is-

lands, then promptly moved to Florida. He knew all about Dr. Buzzard. "I don't believe he was buried at all," he said.

"Cremated?"

"No, cut up and passed around."

Had I been standing on another porch, I would have surely fallen off this time. Recovering, I asked for an explanation.

"Powerful medicine," the artist said. "Can you imagine being a conjureman in possession of a boxful of Dr. Buzzard's metacarpals? You could be elected mayor of Savannah."

My skepticism must have been obvious. The artist named an island funeral parlor, one that had been in business a long, long time. Maybe they had records.

But I was too white to get in the door. The director's wife blocked it with her considerable bulk, demanded the purpose of my visit.

"I'm doing research on old graves in the area."

My ambiguity was not as artful as I had hoped. Though folklorists had long been studying the African retention of decorating graves with the last item used by the departed—cups, bowls, medicine and whiskey bottles, telephones, televisions, sundry small appliances—this woman knew better. "Which one?" she asked.

I continued my transparency. "Stephaney Robinson," I said, using the doctor's legal name.

There was a brief fluttering of an eyelid, the twitch of

a cheek. "Why are you interested in Stephaney Robinson?"

"He was a very famous man."

"By what right was he famous?"

I was increasingly weary of the pointless charade. I blurted, "He was Dr. Buzzard, the most famous root doctor in the world!"

The woman did not even smile.

I rattled on—something like: I am not a practitioner. I do not wish to be mayor of Savannah. I am a journalist. A professional. A folklorist. My interest is academic. . . .

Perhaps. But I was still too white. She cut me off. "Have you spoken with the family?"

Another dead end.

I went back to my father. He again referred me to Warden Incommunicado. I was detailing the pointlessness of that approach when my uncle made an appearance. My uncle had drilled wells for the island folk for fifty years. He knew the strata, geological and social, as well as any man—white man, anyway. He giggled at mention of Dr. Buzzard, began a long recitation of tales I had heard as a child. I listened respectfully, then interrupted with my request.

He didn't know, but a friend might.

Another name, another call. A shrimp captain this time, a man whose age squarely bisected the gulf of years between my father and myself. I got the usual interrogation about my intentions and then the captain directed me to a little Baptist church on a remote corner of St. Helena Is-

land. The grave was marked, he said.

So my friend had been right. They dared not bury the doctor anywhere else.

There was more to the story. The original church had burned, and from his considerable largesse, Dr. Buzzard had built the congregation a new one, from basement to steeple, the captain said.

So *that's* why he is buried there.

But there was more. Certain valuables had been buried with the doctor. Items more valuable than the doctor, himself? "Yes, of considerable value. But I am not at liberty to say more." The captain made a final request: "Leave my name out of this."

I promised I would.

We mounted an evening expedition—two friends, four-wheel drive, camera, notepad, snake stick, chigger spray, flask of good whiskey, shiny new quarter. The first items were necessities, the last two for protocol. Visitations at such places required placation, a token offering, lest some unwanted essence follow you home to demand tribute. Though not a professed believer, I had heard enough, seen enough to know better than to roil those spiritual waters.

The graves, dating from the forties and fifties, formed a narrow row along the south side of the churchyard, a hundred feet in the shade of rustling oaks. But no Stephaney Robinson. Back and forth we walked in the fading light, scanning names, my heart heavier with every step.

Back in the truck again, one friend consoled. "It was not meant to be." The other teased. "He's fooled you again."

The truck began to roll. I took one last quick look in the mirror. "Wait."

The truck lurched to a halt.

I walked back to the graves. The headstones filled the little plot in neat rows, two by two, three by three. But one was missing. There in the center of what should have been a grave, was a small depression, a ten quart hole. A person, or persons, unknown had been gradually removing grave-yard dirt.

One friend brought the camera, the other the whiskey.

I took pictures. Of what? Of the object of my quest, a sandy hole in the St. Helena Island ground.

My friend opened the whiskey, but I bade him put it away. The ambiguity of pouring whiskey on a grave in a Baptist cemetery was too much for me to consider. It might do more harm than good. He passed the flask to me, but I declined. It would be rude to drink without offering it to all parties.

We were back in the truck and two miles away when I remembered the quarter. Uncertain, preoccupied, and per-haps a little fearful, I had forgotten. I took a last look in the mirror, as the truck rocked down the hoven old roadbed, as the oaks closed in overhead, the Spanish moss hanging like long gray strings of tears. And I hoped that I had not found

it after all—that Dr. Buzzard had fooled me once again. For I had taken something. I had taken photographs. I had disturbed the dignity of his sleep. I had circumvented his heirs' desire for anonymity.

And I had left nothing in return.

"Paging Doctor Buzzard . . . ." Though many believers take goofer dust from the unmarked grave (top) to the right of this stone marker, there is another grave (bottom) not five miles away.

Bibliography

Bennett, John. *The Doctor to the Dead*. Columbia, SC: University of South Carolina Press, 1995. A reprint of a 1943 collection of spooky Gullah tales from Charleston, South Carolina, many of them involving conjuration. Most tales have been rendered into modern English, making them comprehensible to those uninitiated to Gullah syntax and pronunciation.

Gonzales, Ambrose E. *The Black Border, Gullah Stories of the Carolina Coast*. Columbia, SC: State Printing, 1964. Reprint of a 1922 classic, reflecting the racial bias of its day. Forty-two stories, many suffering from an unsuccessful attempt to render Gullah dialect into standard English. The vocabulary offered in the appendix is a priceless asset for the serious folklorist.

Holloway, Joseph E., ed. *Africanisms in American Culture*. Bloomington: University of Indiana Press, 1991. A collection of scholarly essays documenting the retention of Africanisms in the United States, some easy reading, others not, all fascinating.

Hyatt, Harry M. *Hoodoo, Conjuration, Witchcraft, Rootwork, Vols. 1 & 2*. Hannibal Western, 1970. Over 2,000 pages of transcribed recordings of interviews with root doctors, conjurists, satisfied and dissatisfied patients. A wealth of information, but unedited, ponderous, often tedious.

Karade, Ifa. *The Handbook of Yoruba Religious Concepts*. York Beach, ME: Weiser, 1994. A concise, very readable summary of the Ifa religion, Africa's oldest and most influential.

McTeer, J.E. *Fifty Years as a Lowcountry Witch Doctor.* Beaufort, SC: Beaufort Book Company, 1976. One of the few white rootworkers tells all. McTeer used conjuration as an adjunct to his duties as sheriff of Beaufort County, trading spells with Dr. Buzzard, the most famed—and feared—root doctor of them all.

———. *The High Sheriff of the Low Country.* Beaufort, SC: Beaufort Book Company, 1970. Anecdotes of law enforcement in Beaufort County, South Carolina.

Puckett, Newbell Niles, and Patterson Smith. *Folk Beliefs of the Southern Negro.* 1968. A reprint of a 1926 study of conjuration throughout the South. Readable but dated with some excellent anecdotes and photographs.

Rosengarten, Theodore. *Tombee, Portrait of a Cotton Planter.* New York: Quill/William Morrow, 1986. The plantation journal of Thomas B. Chaplin (1822-1890) with an extensive commentary by Rosengarten. A must for anyone who wishes to understand the cotton culture and the complex relationships between slaves and their masters.

Towne, Laura M. *The Journal of Laura M. Towne.* New York: Negro Universities Press, 1969. Diary of a Yankee schoolmarm who spent forty years among the Gullah on St. Helena Island.

Usher, Roland G. *The Rise of the American People.* Century, 1916. Long out of print, this classic essay on the meaning of the American experience raises politically incorrect questions about northern involvement in the slave trade, offers some interesting statistics from pre-Civil War census figures.

Index

About the Author

A native of Beaufort, South Carolina, ROGER PINCKNEY is a graduate of the University of South Carolina and the University of Iowa's Writer's Workshop. His articles have appeared in numerous periodicals on American history. He is author of *The Beaufort Chronicles*, a historical guidebook, and *The Right Side of the River: Romance, Rage, and Wonder*, which includes essays of life on Daufuskie Island, the place he now calls home.

CPSIA information can be obtained
at www.ICGtesting.com
Printed in the USA
BVHW050740291021
620153BV00006B/95